ACROSS
THE OUTBACK

READER'S DIGEST

Travels & Adventures

ACROSS
THE OUTBACK

Published by The Reader's Digest Association, Inc.

NEW YORK • MONTREAL • LONDON • SYDNEY • CAPE TOWN

◆ COVER:

Main picture: **Termite mounds rise from the savannah like so many gravestones. These living monuments have been known to measure 18 feet high.**

Smaller pictures, from top to bottom: **During a rest on his epic camel journey, Tom Bergin makes notes in the company of fellow traveller Paddy McHugh. A koala looks out from the branches of a eucalyptus tree. Symbol of Australia, the boomerang is the stock in trade of the Aboriginal hunter. A colourful rainbow lorikeet feeds on the pollen of a Grevillea. The face of an Aboriginal girl, daubed with colourful paints, lights up for the camera.**

Spine: **An Aboriginal dancer from Arnhem Land, dramatically smeared with white body paint.**

◆ FRONTISPIECE:

The baobab, or bottle tree, is a common sight in the Kimberley region of Western Australia. The tree uses its massive trunk for storing water.

◆ TITLE PAGE:

An Aboriginal rock painting of a crocodile, with a stencilled hand below.

◆ OPPOSITE:

Red, orange and iridescent green harlequin bugs hibernate together on a leaf.

◆ CONTENTS PAGES:

Left: **An Aborigine sits contemplatively by a fire, just as his ancestors have done for over 40,000 years. His modern clothing is all that serves to date the scene.**

Right: **During a rest on his epic camel journey, Tom Bergin makes notes in the company of fellow traveller Paddy McHugh.**

◆ PAGES 8–9:

Uluru, or Ayers Rock, fully six miles in circumference, rises red from the surrounding plain. In the distance stand the equally mysterious Olgas.

◆ PAGES 42–43:

A camel caravan heads out across the lonely outback.

ACROSS THE OUTBACK was edited and designed
by The Reader's Digest Association Limited, London.

The Reader's Digest Association Limited
Berkeley Square House, Berkeley Square, London W1X 6AB

In the Steps of Burke and Wills: Original full-length version
by Tom Bergin
published by the Australian Broadcasting Commission
© 1981 by Australian Broadcasting Commission
British condensed version © The Reader's Digest Association Limited, 1995

Contributors

Consultant Editor: Donald Payne

Special Adviser: Earle Bloomfield

Series Editor: Steve Savage

Volume Editor: Charlotte Rundall

Associate Editors: David Blomfield, David Compton

Copy Editor: Elfreda Powell

Research and Editorial Assistance: Julia Bruce

Art Editor: Karen Stewart

Assistant Designer: Stephen Strong

Picture Researcher: Caroline Hensman

Assistant Picture Researcher: Felicity Croydon

Additional material by: Tim Locke, John Man, Keith Spence

Watercolour illustrations: Mark Entwisle

Cartography: Malcolm Porter

Index: Brian Amos

◆ The publishers and project team would like to express their gratitude to the Royal Geographical Society for its ongoing help and advice. They would also like to thank Tom Bergin, the Office of Aboriginal and Torres Strait Islander Affairs, Department of Family Services and Aboriginal and Islander Affairs (Queensland) and the many individuals who have contributed to the preparation of this volume.

Contents

AN AUSTRALIAN CHALLENGE

Condensed from IN THE STEPS OF BURKE AND WILLS by Tom Bergin

— page 42 —

♦ *with special features*:

Index and Acknowledgments

— page 186 —

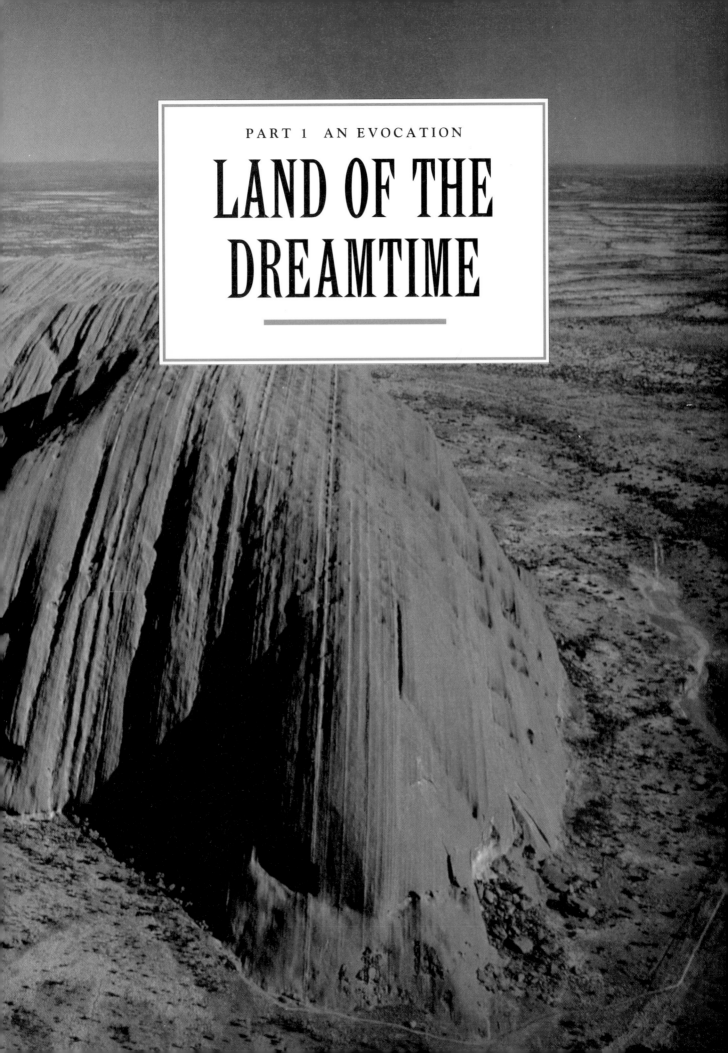

PART 1 AN EVOCATION

LAND OF THE DREAMTIME

Land of the Dreamtime

AUSTRALIA IS A VAST AND ANCIENT LAND, sparsely populated and with huge distances separating its comparatively few cities. The distance between Perth, for instance, and the next major city, Adelaide, is greater than the distance from London to Moscow; while Australia's cattle stations, such as the 12,000-square-mile Anna Creek Station in South Australia, are the largest in the world. So much about Australia—its droughts, its floods, its bushfires—is on a monumental scale.

The same could be said of its age. For although this island continent is ringed with cities which are among the most modern and prosperous in the world, in its central reaches, known as the outback, you will find some of the oldest rocks on Earth. These, scientists tell us, were formed when the crust of our planet was in its infancy and contain tiny mineral grains that are 4,300 million years old—the oldest known objects in the world. No wonder those who visit the outback are awed by its aura of unchanging grandeur: an aura accentuated by its strange plants and creatures, many unique to Australia, and its evocative rock paintings drawn by a people whose culture was already old when Tutankhamun was buried in the Valley of the Kings. This is the Aborigines' Land of the Dreamtime: sacred terrain which, they believe, was not only created by their ancestors but was formed by their bodies.

The story of how this harshly beautiful land was formed and peopled, therefore, begins over 4,000 million years ago.

A World Apart

There are two versions of how life came to Australia. Some Aborigines believe that in the beginning the Earth lay dark and silent, and the Father Spirit was saddened because there was no life on it. In a cave beneath the Nullarbor Plain slept a beautiful woman, the Sun; and the Father Spirit woke her and begged her

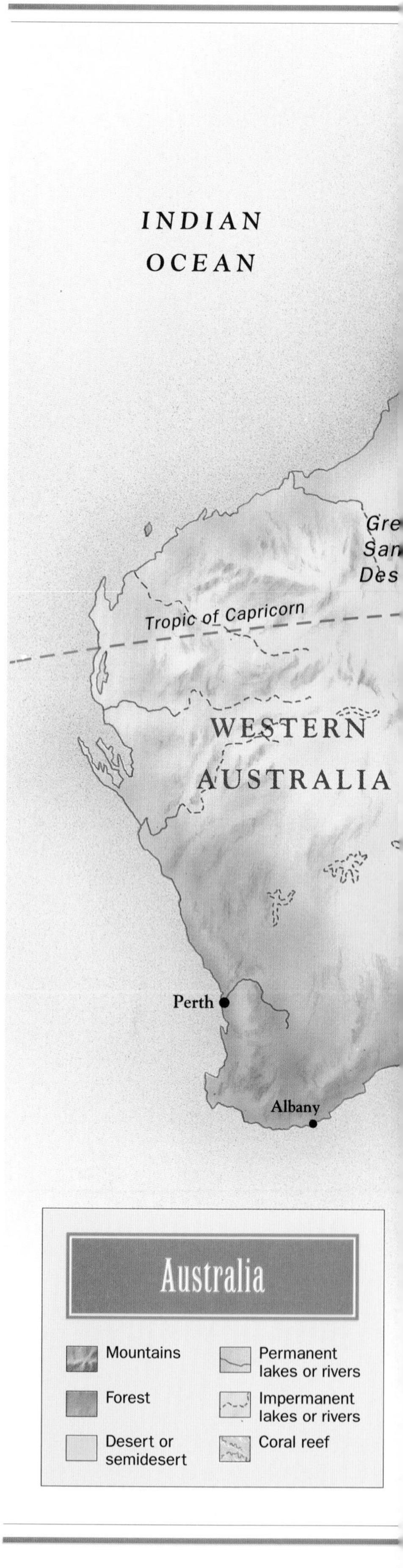

Tropic of Capricorn

Gre
San
Des

WESTERN
AUSTRALIA

Perth

Albany

Australia

Mountains	Permanent lakes or rivers
Forest	Impermanent lakes or rivers
Desert or semidesert	Coral reef

Port Essington

Arafura Sea

Timor Sea

Torres Strait

NEW
GUINEA

Darwin

Kakadu
National
Park

Arnhem
Land

*Gulf of
Carpentaria*

Cape
York
Peninsula

Coral Sea

NORTHERN
TERRITORY

G R E A T   D I V I D E

Great Barrier Reef

A U S T R A L I A

QUEENSLAND

MACDONNELL
RANGES

•Alice Springs

bson Desert

The Olgas ▲ ▲ Uluru (Ayers Rock)

*Simpson
Desert*

Great Artesian

Basin

GREAT DIVIDE

Fraser
Island

Great Victoria Desert

*Sturt
Stony
Desert*

Cooper Creek

Lake
Eyre

Jimbour•

Brisbane•

SOUTH AUSTRALIA

Lake
Torrens

Lake
Frome

Darling

NEW
SOUTH
WALES

Nullarbor Plain

Bathurst•

BLUE MTS.

•Sydney

Botany Bay

Great Australian Bight

Adelaide•

CANBERRA

Murray

AUSTRALIAN
▲ CAPITAL TERRITORY

Mt. Kosciusko

VICTORIA

Melbourne•

Cape Everard
(Hicks Point)

SOUTHERN OCEAN

Bass Strait

TASMANIA

•Hobart

0   200   400 miles

0   200   400 kilometres

to bring the Earth to life. The Sun opened her eyes. And as her rays spread over the land the darkness disappeared, and in the billabongs the sand and the water mated to create life.

Scientists are less poetic. They argue that the ancient rocks of Australia have traversed the Earth from pole to pole, as the giant plates which make up the crust of our planet jostled for position. Australia was part of the huge supercontinent Gondwana until it broke up, and the parts we now know as India, Africa and South America began to move into their present positions, while Australia and Antarctica remained locked together in the south. Finally, about 50 million years ago, Australia broke free of its neighbour and began to move north. It has remained isolated ever since: a world apart.

The Australia which broke free from Antarctica was very different from the Australia of today. Tasmania was joined to the mainland and in the centre of the continent was a large inland sea. Most of the rest was covered by lush temperate forest. Only as the island continent continued to head north did the rainfall decrease, bringing about a gradual deterioration: to woodland, then scrub, then grassland and finally desert. Such changes, however, were slight compared to cataclysmic events taking place in other parts of the world. Huge mountain ranges such as the Himalayas and the Andes were levered up tens of thousands of feet above sea level and, during the ice ages, massive ice caps ground over the polar regions. Isolated Australia, drifting northwards, escaped these traumas, and apart from some volcanic activity and uplift along its eastern edge, was tectonically stable. This, combined with millions of years of erosion, has made Australia the lowest and flattest of the continents, its landscape being sculpted by wind and rain rather than by violent upheaval. Few places over the last million or so years have changed as little as Australia: hence the aura of timelessness that broods over its lonely deserts and plains.

Trees and Flowers from a Vanished World

Many of the plants which we think of as typically Australian originated in the disintegrated supercontinent of Gondwana. However, they are not—as has sometimes been claimed— 'living fossils'; they are species which have adapted in isolation to a changing environment. Some have had to alter little. The king fern for example, now restricted to a few small pockets in Queensland and Fraser Island, is virtually identical to a fossilised tree fern of 65 million years ago. In some other isolated areas ancient palmlike cycads and Kauri pines have survived almost unaltered for some 200 million years.

▲ The rounded 'heads' of the Olgas rise abruptly from the plains and cast dramatic shadows in the evening sun.

▲ Rainwater combines with chemicals in the granite to leave dark streaks on the surface of aptly named Wave Rock.

▲ Skiers tackle the lower slopes of mountains in
Kosciusko National Park, New South Wales, named after
Australia's loftiest peak, Mount Kosciusko.

A Land of Extremes

FOR MANY PEOPLE Australia at once brings to
mind the arid outback. This vast swathe of
parched land stretches across fully two thirds of
the country, interrupted periodically by peculiar
outcrops of giant, weathered rocks rising abruptly
from the monotonous plains. One such outcrop
is the Olgas in the Northern Territory; with their
strange, rounded forms, shaped by wind and rain,
it is easy to see why the Aborigines called the
Olgas *Katatjuta*, or 'many heads'.

Weathering of another sort created the bizarre
formation in Western Australia known as Wave
Rock, which looks like a petrified breaker
permanently poised to crash down on the land
beneath it. Made of granite formed some 2,700
million years ago, Wave Rock was once buried
beneath the ground. Gradually, acids in the soil
ate away at the granite surface to produce an
extraordinary curve, which was exposed when
rainwater washed away the soil.

Yet these timeless monuments to a harsh
environment coexist with another, less familiar,
Australia. For the country's coastal regions where
the outback ends could not be more different.
In eastern Australia, particularly in Queensland
and the coastal regions of the Northern Territory,
high rainfall combines with year-round warm
temperatures to foster rain forests containing
as many as 100 different kinds of tree in little
more than an acre. And within the borders of just
one state—New South Wales—outback and rain
forest coexist with the snow-clad peaks of the
Snowy Mountains, home to the 7,316-foot Mount
Kosciusko, Australia's highest mountain.

▲ **Desert and rain forest
are sometimes only
a few hundred miles
apart in Australia. This
lush glade is in New
South Wales, one of the
most varied of all the
Australian states.**

Spinifex clumps grow outwards in ever-widening rings, while older growth dies off in the middle. The roots reach phenomenal depths in search of water.

A Unique Flora

OVER 90 PER CENT of Australia's native plant species grow naturally nowhere else in the world, a statistic that bears testimony to the continent's long-standing geographic isolation. Australian plants are remarkable, however, not only for their uniqueness but also for the way they have adapted to an often harsh environment.

The ubiquitous eucalypts or gum trees (so-called because of their sticky secretions) conserve precious water and nutrients in hard, evergreen leaves. Many varieties—and there are over 500 of them— are also resistant to fire: the ghost gum, for example, has shiny bark which reflects the heat. Using another survival strategy, spinifex grass combines hard, spiny leaves with roots that reach down 40 feet in search of moisture. The bizarre-looking Sturt's desert pea also has a deep taproot, and in response to rainfall it rapidly sends out yards of furry tentacles across the desert surface to nourish extravagant red and black flowers.

Australia is not all dry, however. In the far southwest high rainfall and humidity are enjoyed by the Albany pitcher plant, but the soil is poor, so the plant compensates by adding flies and other unwary insects to its diet. And on the north and east coasts lie remnants of a rain forest that millions of years ago covered most of the continent. Here, the spectacular flame tree adds an unexpected burst of colour to the surrounding greenery.

The vivid red flowers of the flame tree contrast spectacularly with a bright blue sky. The tree's branches play host to a variety of other plants. ▼

The ghost gum's shimmering white bark protects the tree from the heat of the sun and of bushfires. This tree is growing out of a most unlikely spot!

Sturt's desert pea produces dramatic flowers whose black centres look almost like eyes scanning the sands.

Unwary insects slip helplessly into the 'pitchers' of the Albany pitcher plant to provide it with extra nutrients.

But Australia's most successful tree, the eucalyptus or gum tree, has changed a great deal. It first appeared about 35 million years ago and swiftly colonised Australia by diversifying into an amazing number of habitats. Today there are over 500 different types of eucalypt in Australia, ranging from the magnificent 300-foot Australian mountain ash—the tallest hardwood in the world—to the stunted three foot desert mallee. Some spend the winter encased in ice; some have evolved white bark to cope with high temperatures; some put down vertical roots in saltwater swamps, and some put down horizontal roots in the desert. Many of them shed their bark but not their drooping, grey–green, resinous and sweet-smelling leaves.

Eucalypts are not particularly famous for their flowers but other native Australian plants produce some of the most beautiful and idiosyncratic flowers in the world: huge spectacular bottlebrushes; furry kangaroo paws; flamboyant, fast-growing Sturt's desert peas; orchids some of which grow 40 feet long while others grow entirely underground, and the fire-dependent banksias. Cultured varieties of these beautiful plants often grace Australia's suburban streets and gardens.

But perhaps most beautiful of all are the flowers of the desert. For year after year parts of the outback lie waterless and barren. But after one of the infrequent but heavy rainstorms, brilliant mulla, desert peas and parakeelya burst through the sand and transform the wilderness into a riot of colour. The seeds of many of these plants are coated with a water-soluble chemical, which prevents their germinating until sufficient rain has fallen to ensure that the plant will be able to complete its life cycle—an example of the sort of adaptation Australian flora has had to make to cope with its demanding environment.

Survivors in a Harsh Land

Australian fauna has had to be adaptable too, for the continent offers few easy habitats—nothing like the conditions of plenty enjoyed by insects in a South American rain forest or herbivores on the African plains. This demanding terrain combined with a long isolation has led to the evolution of many species unique to Australia. Huge birds that can't fly and tiny mouse-like creatures that can; strange animals that hop rather than walk and carry their prematurely born young in pouches. No wonder Joseph Banks, botanist on Cook's first voyage, spoke of a treasure trove of strange creatures. Yet—as was the case with Australia's plants—these are not relics from a bygone age, but creatures which, in isolation, have developed particular characteristics to cope with their environment.

Some types of goanna can grow to seven feet long, and are among the largest predators in Australia.

AUSTRALIA has often been described as an 'island ark'. When it drifted away from Antarctica and into isolation 50 million years ago, it carried with it an assortment of wild animals, dominated by reptiles and marsupials. For the next 40 million years, until Australia finally drifted within reach of Southeast Asia, these creatures lived and developed in a world apart. No wonder the first European explorers were amazed by their strangeness.

One of the first peculiarities the Europeans would have observed was the lack of large predatory mammals. Where Africa had its lions and India its tigers, Australia's only sizeable native predators were reptiles—crocodiles where there was water, and seven-foot-long goannas, or monitor lizards, on the vast deserts of the interior. When the explorers came across the duck-billed platypus, though, they were even more surprised, for here was a creature that seemed to be part reptile and part mammal, with the weirdest hotchpotch of features imaginable. The platypus is, in fact, one of the few remaining examples of the monotreme order of mammals,

◀ Reptile or mammal? The furry, web-footed, duck-billed platypus is in fact a rare and ancient type of mammal.

which experts reckon first appeared on Earth 120 million years ago.

Just as unusual are the marsupials, which include, among other animals, many different species of kangaroo and wallaby, as well as koalas and possums. These varied-looking mammals share one unusual feature: they all give birth to minute, premature young—little bigger than a thumbnail. Marsupial mothers nurse their young from teats either in a protective pouch or in a depression on their belly.

Australia's skies are filled with hundreds of species of birds, which are no less varied than its earthbound animals. However, probably the best-known of these cannot fly at all: instead, emus and their equally bizarre relatives, cassowaries, run on enormously long legs that help elevate them to a height of up to six feet!

▲ Northeastern Australia's rain forests are home to the southern cassowary, which, like the emu, cannot fly.

A baby koala clings to its mother after venturing from the safety of her pouch in search of eucalyptus leaves. ▼

◀ Eastern grey kangaroos enjoy the sea air at a deserted New South Wales beach. Like most marsupials, kangaroos nurture their young in pouches (inset). The young are less than an inch long when born, and develop in the pouch over a period of up to 11 months.

The kangaroos and the platypuses are examples of these specialised mammals. Most mammals are placental—that is to say their young are nourished in the womb and born more or less fully developed. Kangaroos, however, along with the majority of Australia's mammals, are marsupial, which is to say that their young are born unformed and are invariably nurtured in a pouch; although mature red kangaroos are about the size of a human being, their babies at birth are minute. There are over 50 species of kangaroo, ranging from the magnificent red, well over five feet tall, to the tiny rat-kangaroo, less than one foot tall. All have powerful hind legs and these enable the larger species to cover up to 30 feet in a single bound, and to keep going for long distances at almost 30 miles an hour.

Even more amazing are the platypuses. These shy and playful creatures are monotremes, a rare type of mammal that lays eggs. There are only two sorts of monotremes left in the world, the land-dwelling spiny anteater or echidna, with types native to both Australia and New Guinea, and the water-dwelling platypus found only in Australia. The latter have so many apparently contradictory component parts that the early specimens sent back to Europe for analysis were thought to be fakes, stitched together by a practical joker. For they are furry, warm-blooded mammals that lay eggs, lactate, and spend much of their life underwater. They have webbed feet equipped with poisonous spurs, tails like beavers and bills like ducks. At one time threatened with extinction, they are now a protected species.

There are over 700 species of birds in Australia. Most successful are the 50-odd types of parrot. These flamboyantly coloured birds are widespread throughout the continent, occurring in rain forest and desert as well as woodland and grassland. They even flourish in city centres: a reminder to Australians that the exotica of the outback are ever on their doorstep.

The Coming of Man

Man came surprisingly early to Australia. During the last Ice Age sea levels were far lower than they are today, creating an almost continuous land bridge between Australia and the mainland of Southeast Asia. And it was almost certainly Southeast Asia from which the first Australians came, 45,000 to 60,000 years ago. When the Ice Age ended, the sea levels rose and these first Australians, whom we know as Aborigines, became cut off from the rest of the world.

By about 10,000 BC the Aborigines had colonised the whole of their new-found land, and had fragmented into something like 700 tribal units. Along the coast and in fertile inland areas like the Murray–Darling Basin a tribe might spend part of each year in the same place; but in the outback they were forever on the move, trekking from one waterhole to the next, exhausting one meagre supply of food before moving on to another. They had no homes, no crops, no clothes and few possessions; also they had no chiefs, being ruled by tribal elders who were the upholders of traditional lore. The few things that they did have they shared: food and family, children and laughter, danger and thirst; their children hardly ever cried, and they cared for their old and their sick. One of the first Europeans to make contact with them, Lieutenant, later Captain, James Cook, wrote perspicaciously: 'To some they may appear to be the most wretched people on earth, but in reality [they] are far more happier than we Europeans…They live in Tranquillity…The Earth and the sea of their own accord furnishes them with all things necessary for life'. Long before the arrival of white men, the Aborigines had explored every nook and cranny of their continent, had found every waterhole, crossed every saltpan and climbed every desiccated peak.

Because they spent their entire lives ultimately reliant upon a particular area of land and drawing sustenance from it, it was almost inevitable that they should become bound to their land by ties both physical and spiritual. Aborigines don't merely believe that their gods created the land, they believe that their gods *are* the land. 'The Australian Aborigine does not transplant,' writes the anthropologist Colin Simpson. 'His altars are waterholes, hills and rocks. He is, by the nature of his beliefs, identified with and bound to a particular patch of earth, his tribal land.' If you take away a Christian's or a Buddhist's or a Hindu's land, you don't take away his faith. But Aborigines dispossessed of their land are dispossessed also of the essential element in their belief; which explains why many of these people, when driven from their tribal land and forced to live on the periphery of towns and cities, felt they had nothing left to live for, and sought refuge in suicide, petty crime and alcohol. Only in recent decades have efforts been made to restore to them their land, and thus their faith and their dignity.

The First Europeans

The Chinese *may* have seen Australia in the 15th century and the Portuguese *may* have seen it in the 16th; but the first fully authenticated sighting took place in 1606 when the Dutch navigator, Willem Jansz, passed through the Torres Strait and landed at the northernmost tip of Queensland. This was followed by a spate of further sightings.

▲ Aborigines like this man from the Tanami Desert in the Northern Territory are keeping alive traditions that go back tens of thousands of years.

This cave painting depicts the legendary brothers who fought so violently over a woman that they created thunder and lightning. ▼

Some Aboriginal rock carvings may be 45,000 years old. Many depict animals, while others, like these at Ewaninga in the Northern Territory, are more abstract.

The First Australians

NOBODY KNOWS for certain when the ancestors of today's Aborigines first came to Australia. Some experts think it was over 100,000 years ago, but most agree that it was probably between 45,000 and 60,000 years ago, during the last Ice Age. They would have crossed by boat from Southeast Asia as far as New Guinea, and from there would simply have walked to the main continent via a land bridge exposed when sea levels dropped.

Even if all that happened at the later date of 45,000 years ago, Aboriginal culture is still the oldest continuing culture on Earth. What is more, it is unique in having remained virtually unchanged throughout its long history, right up until the time Europeans started colonising Australia in the 18th century. The Aborigines must have appeared very primitive to those first settlers, for many wore no clothes, and lived off the land as hunter-gatherers.

However, their way of life was far from simple, for they lived in structured social groups, with profound religious beliefs and a highly developed artistic tradition. Indeed, the oldest rock carvings in the world are Aboriginal, dating back tens of thousands of years, and many Australian caves are decorated with elaborate paintings, evoking legendary heroes and myths.

This rich and ancient culture was threatened with destruction when European settlers arrived, and for the next 200 years Aborigines fought for its survival. Many have now abandoned the struggle and with it their traditional ways; however, those who keep their traditions going are safeguarding a unique heritage for the future.

Europeans viewed the Aborigines as utterly primitive. This 19th-century watercolour by W.R. Govett shows 'simple savages' making fire.

James Cook (1728–79), seen here in a portrait by Nathaniel Dance, rose from humble origins to become one of the greatest seamen of all time, an expert in navigation and astronomy and also a highly skilled surveyor and cartographer. He was the first person to chart Australia's east coast.

IN AUGUST 1768, a small but sturdy vessel named *Endeavour*, commanded by one Lieutenant James Cook, set sail from Plymouth, England, bound for the Pacific island of Tahiti. Its mission: to observe the transit of the planet Venus across the Sun. The Royal Society, which sponsored the trip, hoped that these observations would greatly assist future navigational calculations.

Cook, however, had another secret set of instructions, given him by the Admiralty: he was to travel on from Tahiti in search of land. It was widely held in Europe that a vast continent stretched across the bottom of the world to counterbalance the landmasses of the north. Whichever European power gained sovereignty over that land would gain a massive strategic advantage and sole rights to its natural resources.

Cook duly sailed on after making his observations in Tahiti. He circumnavigated New Zealand's two islands, and headed west. Land was

sighted again. At last *Endeavour* put in at a sheltered bay, and the British flag was hoisted. The scientific party Cook had brought with him, headed by botanist Joseph Banks, excitedly collected specimens of the abundant exotic flora they found; Cook would later name the place Botany Bay in recognition of Banks's work.

As the *Endeavour* continued up the east coast, Cook became convinced that this was the same continent that Dutch sailors had first observed from the north and west over 150 years earlier—New Holland, they had called it, and they had found it so barren and inhospitable they had passed on. Cook by contrast had found that the east coast supported a wealth of life. His dramatic news nearly failed to reach home when the *Endeavour* was holed on the Great Barrier Reef, but the resourceful crew repaired her and she soldiered on, rounding Cape York in the far northeast before returning to England with the triumphant news.

Sydney Parkinson made exquisite sketches of the Australian flora at Botany Bay. This evergreen shrub was named *Banksia serrata* after Joseph Banks, head of Cook's scientific party.

Only once in her long voyage did the *Endeavour* spring a leak, after running aground on the Great Barrier Reef; but the crew careened her, as shown here, and repaired the hull.

In April 1770, Cook made his historic landing at Botany Bay, and claimed the continent for Britain. The historic moment was captured here by Samuel Calvert (1828–1913).

The Dutch were excellent traders who built up a great 'empire of spices' based on Batavia (present-day Jakarta on the island of Java). At first they used to reach Batavia by sailing northeast from Cape Town across the Indian Ocean; but they discovered that by keeping to a more southerly route they could pick up the strong winds of the Roaring Forties and make passage in half the time. This new route led them to the west coast of Australia. During the early 17th century Dutch ships made several landfalls along this coast which they named New Holland. They found a lee shore, an arid hinterland, and no easy pickings for trade. They therefore made no attempt to settle in the land they had discovered, but used it merely as a turning point *en route* to Batavia.

The first Europeans to sight eastern Australia were the crew of HMS *Endeavour,* commanded by James Cook. In three great voyages between 1768 and 1779 Cook redrew the map of the southern hemisphere. He disproved the myth of the Great Southern Continent, or *Terra Australis Incognita,* which for hundreds of years people had thought must exist to counterbalance the great landmasses of the north; although he never sighted Antarctica he delineated its possible extent—smaller than previously supposed—by sailing round it close to the Antarctic Circle. He circumnavigated and surveyed New Zealand and discovered the east coast of Australia. On April 19, 1770, the crew of the *Endeavour,* heading west from New Zealand, sighted land which Cook named Hicks Point (now Cape Everard), about 250 miles east of Melbourne. Cook followed the coastline northwards until he came to a promising-looking bay. Here he put ashore; and the expedition's naturalist, Joseph Banks, and his assistants soon collected over 200 plants unknown in Europe, hence the name 'Botany Bay'. The *Endeavour* then sailed north, sometimes outside the Great Barrier Reef and sometimes inside it. On one occasion she was within the width of a single wave of being swept to destruction on the outer edge of the reef. On another, *Endeavour* grounded on jagged coral, which ripped open her hull. However, Cook and his well-disciplined crew managed to careen their stricken ship near the mouth of a river—later named the Endeavour—and carry out repairs. During their six weeks ashore they were able to study the terrain, and Cook's report was discerning: 'The Countrie is well diversified. The soil of the hills is dry and stoney and produceth thin grass and a little wood; that of the plains is friable and produceth long grass and shrubs. It is indifferently well watered with many Brooks but no great Rivers. The Climate is warm and fine and the air wholesom.'

From Transportation to Transformation

BRITAIN WAS IN TROUBLE when the Americans signed their Declaration of Independence in 1776. She had lost not only her colonies and their trading potential, but also a convenient dumping ground for inmates of her overcrowded gaols.

A solution to both problems emerged in 1779 when Joseph Banks—the scientist who had accompanied James Cook on his voyage to Australia 11 years earlier—suggested to the government that they establish a trading colony on the land Cook had claimed for Britain. The authorities were quick to recognise that such a place, on the far side of the world, would also make an ideal penal colony.

So the historic First Fleet of 11 ships, carrying 772 convicts and their Royal Marine guards, set sail in 1787 under the command of Captain Arthur Phillip. After an arduous eight-month voyage, the fleet dropped anchor in Botany Bay, and before long Phillip had established the first settlement at nearby Port Jackson—present-day Sydney. Prisons soon sprang up as far afield as Tasmania,

and the brutality with which some were ruled became legendary. But times were hard even for non-prisoners: crops failed, cattle turned wild and supplies from England could not be relied upon.

Eventually matters improved as prosperity increased and the colony started to attract free settlers. They and ex-convicts alike became the farmers, builders and explorers of a new nation, their entrepreneurial spirit transforming Britain's farthest-flung outpost. Australia became a land of opportunity.

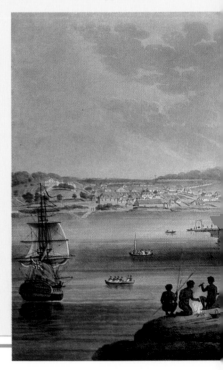

▲ Joseph Banks (1743–1820) has been called 'the father of Australia', for it was he who first suggested establishing a colony there.

◄ Pioneers of the new nation, pictured outside their humble shack.

Old world meets new: Port Jackson (the site of modern Sydney) in 1804, overlooked by an Aboriginal family. ▶

▲ Port Arthur prison in Tasmania was notorious for the brutality of its officers.

As this engraving shows, convicts were locked in cramped cages for the eight-month voyage to Australia. ▼

It was Cook's account, backed up by Banks's more detailed observations and recommendations, which persuaded the British authorities that 'this most convenient southland' was suitable for colonisation.

The Penal Settlements

Britain's loss of the American states in the War of Independence (1775–83) provided two groups of potential colonists for New South Wales, as Cook had called the east coast of Australia. A number of New World farmers had lost their land during the war, and Joseph Banks had already reported to the House of Commons in 1779 on the suitability of the new land for colonisation. But the American farmers proved loath to be shipped to the opposite side of the world. One of Cook's officers, James Matra, after discussions with Banks, suggested that convicts be sent instead, as America was no longer available as a convenient place of exile for them.

In May 1787 the first convict fleet left England for Botany Bay: two warships, three supply ships and six transports. The crews and escort numbered 233 and the convicts 772, including 191 women and 13 children. In command was Captain Arthur Phillip: it was due largely to his ability and humanity that the voyage was completed with just 23 casualties. The tedium must have been mind-boggling: sailing for 250 days 'over a vast and imperfectly explor'd sea with not so much as a fish or a bird for company'. Only as they entered the Great Australian Bight was the monotony broken. They met a vast herd of black whales, which kept pace with the ships for hour after hour. It was a prophetic meeting. For the convicts and the whales were, between them, to ensure the founding of Australia.

The harbour at Botany Bay was exposed and there was no water supply. Searching for an alternative site, Phillip found one a few miles north. This was Port Jackson, named, but not explored, by Cook in 1770. 'We have had the satisfaction,' wrote Phillip, 'of finding what is surely the finest harbour in the world, in which 1,000 ships of the line might ride in safety. It has sweet Water, and numerous sheltered Coves.' In one of these coves Phillip was met by some Aborigines who waded into the water and examined his boat. 'Their manly behaviour,' he wrote, 'made me give this place the name of Manly Cove'.

Port Jackson, later renamed Sydney, was a fine site but the settlement didn't take root easily. Within a week of Phillip's arrival 'sickness and scurvy were raging in a manner most extraordinary'—significantly one of the first buildings the settlers erected was a hospital. Other troubles followed. The colonists

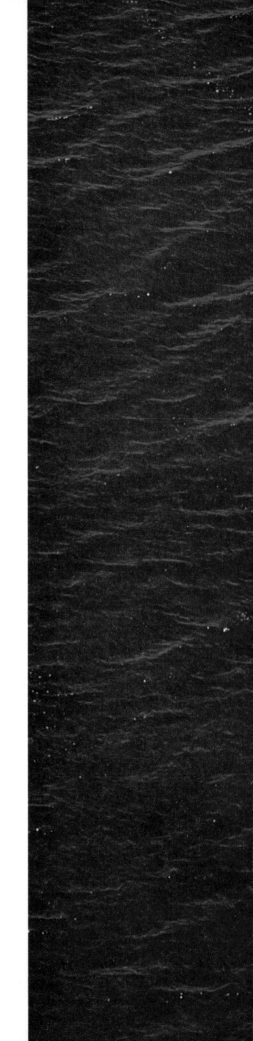

were inadequately equipped and few had much practical knowledge of agriculture. The soil was poor; their livestock died; their seeds were eaten by ants and their crops succumbed to insects, fungi and bacteria to which they had no immunity. The colony nearly starved when a shipwreck halted supplies from Britain. But, after about a decade, thanks largely to Phillip and a handful of dedicated men, the survival of this small community was assured. There is, however, a world of difference between survival and prosperity; and the latter came first not from the arid pastures of the coastal plains, but from the richer pastures of the sea.

Harvest of the Sea

It is difficult for us today to appreciate how important the whaling industry was in the 18th and 19th centuries. Before the use of chemical oils and electricity, it was whale oil which lubricated the machines of the industrial revolution and whale oil that lit homes and streets throughout the world. And it was whalebone, or baleen—flexible bonelike filters from the whale's mouth—that was used to make the corsets and stays essential to women of fashion. In about 1800 the bones of an average-sized whale fetched over £2,000 (the equivalent of at least £100,000 in today's currency). No wonder the luckless creatures were soon hunted to near-extinction in the northern hemisphere, and the whalers of Europe and America were obliged to seek their quarry elsewhere.

The first convict fleet to sail to Australia had sighted whales. Subsequent fleets came equipped with harpoons, and invariably met large numbers of black whales off the South Australian coast. These 60-foot, 60-ton, peaceful, slow-moving creatures were so easy to kill and provided such high quality blubber and baleen that they were proclaimed the 'right' whales to kill. The name stuck, and right whales became part of Australia's history.

Southeast Australia lies on the migratory route of the right whales, and in winter vast herds of these playful and gregarious creatures flocked into the coastal waters of Victoria, South Australia and Tasmania. They often disrupted shipping, and made so much noise that the governor of Tasmania complained they kept him awake with their 'snoring'.

Initially, whale ships operated from Sydney; but they soon found other suitable harbours and it wasn't long before literally

Right whales, like this pair, carefully guarding a youngster, are no longer the 'right' whales to hunt, as the species has been protected since 1935. In the 19th century, though, they were killed in their thousands. ▶

hundreds of whaling stations were springing up along a coast that up to now had been known only to the Aborigines. For the indigenous people of Tasmania this was a death knell. They got in the Europeans' way. So their waterholes were poisoned with arsenic, and they were hunted to death with packs of dogs. Within 80 years of the whalers' arrival, not a single Aborigine was left in Tasmania.

The whaling settlements, however, prospered. Everyone knows about the convicts sent 'down under', but statistics confirm that they were few compared to the whalers who came here voluntarily. In 1800, at a critical time for the settlements, there were 936 naval and military personnel and free settlers in the continent, 1,977 convicts and 3,584 whalers.

'One land, to which I give the name Australia'

In 1801 Matthew Flinders, a young naval officer, was given command of HMS *Investigator* and told 'thoroughly to examine the lands of New Holland and New South Wales', which many still believed to be two islands. In spite of his ship being old and leaking like a sieve—she was all that could be spared for exploration during the Napoleonic Wars—Flinders set sail from England and made a safe landfall off southwest Australia to begin his survey of an unknown coastline on which few Europeans had set foot. The result was so accurate that Flinders's charts were still in use at the end of the Second World War; while a valuable bonus was the work of his naturalist Robert Brown and his artist Ferdinand Bauer. During their frequent forays ashore along the south coast, the meticulous Brown collected and classified 750 grasses and plants of which 350 were previously unknown, while the gifted Bauer completed beautiful paintings of over 450 animals and plants.

After repairs and provisioning in Port Jackson, as Sydney was still known, Flinders surveyed the east coast as precisely as the south. His troubles began when he came to the north coast. The climate here is damp and unhealthy, and his crew (who had been at sea for over 18 months) succumbed to a variety of tropical fevers, while his leaking ship began to fall apart. Flinders ran her aground in the Gulf of Carpentaria, hoping to recaulk her; but this proved impossible. It seemed that he had little hope of returning to Port Jackson through the heavy seas of the Pacific and the hazards of the Great Barrier Reef, and his best bet would be to continue round through the quieter waters of the Indian Ocean and the Great Australian Bight. He succeeded, but only after a nightmare voyage. By the time he limped into Port Jackson, nearly a third of his ship's company

Ferdinand Bauer (1760–1840) excelled in the depiction of such exotic creatures as this colourful red rosella parrot. ▼

Paintings like this one by William Westall (1781–1850) must have fired the imagination of Europeans who had not yet visited the new continent. ▶

Even celebrated animal artist George Stubbs (1724–1806) struggled with the unfamiliar form of the kangaroo—especially as his only model was a stuffed skin brought home by Cook! ▼

First Impressions

FEW PEOPLE in the history of the world have enjoyed the privilege of being the first to set foot on a land completely unknown to them, and of feeling the sense of sheer wonderment that such an experience must produce. For the Europeans who first came to Australia, the experience must have been doubly astounding, so strange and unfamiliar were the animals and people they found there. Of the kangaroo, Joseph Banks, the scientist on James Cook's voyage to Australia between 1768–70, wrote: 'To compare it to any European animal would be impossible as it has not the least resemblance of any one I have seen.'

Words, then, failed Banks—and many others like him; the only alternative way to convey the strangeness of Australia to people back home was through pictures. Even this medium, however, had its difficulties, as artists grappled with forms they had never encountered in the confines of their drawing classes. Some, however, got to grips with the unfamiliar subjects remarkably well, including William Westall and Ferdinand Bauer, who both accompanied Matthew Flinders on his arduous

Watpipa the „Old Man„, our guide on Sep. 24. 6°
L Becker.

▲ **An elderly Aborigine drawn by Ludwig Becker (1808–1861) on Burke and Wills's expedition.**

circumnavigation of Australia in 1801. Westall captured beautifully the unique strangeness of the countryside and the Aborigines who inhabited it, and Bauer produced exquisite drawings and paintings of exotic flora and fauna, which rightly found their way to some of Europe's finest museums.

Westall and Bauer were lucky—Flinders's expedition was a success. Another expedition artist, Ludwig Becker, was not so fortunate, and died a lingering death from scurvy on the ill-fated Burke and Wills crossing of Australia in 1860; only his poignant, delicate sketches survived to tell his story.

had died, another third were so weak they couldn't stand, and the *Investigator* was declared 'not worth repairing'. So rotten were her timbers that a piece of bamboo could be pushed clean through them.

When he tried to return home, in HMS *Porpoise*, Flinders was shipwrecked and his papers were damaged. On his second attempt he was captured by the French and imprisoned for seven years in Mauritius. When he was released he was a sick man. He devoted his last years to writing an account of his expedition, the magnificent *Voyage to Terra Australis*. But he never saw his great work, dying the day after it was published.

Posterity has been kinder to Flinders. Today his is the most common place name to be found in Australia. In the preface to his book he wrote what has proved an enduring epitaph: 'Now that New Holland and New South Wales are known to form one land, there must be a general name [given] to the whole. I have ventured to readopt the original Terra Australis. Had I permitted myself any change it would have been to convert Australis to Australia.'

Breakthrough: Across the Great Divide

The soil around Sydney is sandy and not very fertile, and the early settlers were soon searching for better pastures. The Blue Mountains, part of the Great Divide, blocked their path. From the coastal plain these look like heavily wooded hills; but in fact their cliffs are an escarpment, the eastern edge of the huge plateau-cum-plain that stretches across Australia. This formidable obstacle defeated all attempts to penetrate it for 25 years. Then, instead of trying to push directly through the valleys, three farmers—Gregory Blaxland, William Wentworth and Lieutenant William Lawson—set out to tackle the escarpment by keeping to the ridges; these were high, narrow and complex, but they were also comparatively flat and free from scrub. In three weeks they covered 60 miles, emerging into promising, well-wooded grassland.

The Governor, Lachlan Macquarie, sent his deputy surveyor, George Evans, and a team of bushmen and convicts to follow in the farmers' tracks; and they pushed west to the Bathurst Plains. 'I cannot speak too highly of [this] country,' wrote Evans. 'The soil is exceeding rich and produces the finest grass.' Macquarie ordered a road to be built across the mountains and soon settlers

◄ The Three Sisters—these dramatic stone pinnacles—and the dense eucalyptus scrub below make it easy to see why the Blue Mountains proved such an obstacle to settlers. The range was named after the blue haze that hangs over it, created by airborne droplets of eucalyptus oil.

▲ These merino rams, their faces almost lost in great folds of wool, are fine specimens of Australia's most popular breed.

A farmer's hands reveal the merino's fine, dense fleece. ▶

◀ Sheepshearers like these have the daunting annual task of shearing the nation's 150 million sheep.

Sheep—The Impetus for Exploration

STRANGE AS IT MAY SEEM to the uninitiated, there are nine times as many sheep in Australia as people—150 million, in fact, or 15 per cent of all the sheep in the world! Sheep farming is self-evidently one of the biggest businesses in the country, and its history is one of the great success stories of the country.

The first sheep arrived in New South Wales with the early settlers, on the convict fleets of the late 18th century. Many died during the long passage, but a shrewd young lieutenant, John Macarthur, bought some of the survivors and set about breeding from them. Macarthur's sheep would have won no prizes today, but he soon bought some merinos, renowned for their fine fleeces, and crossbred them with more resilient types better able to withstand the hot climate and rough grazing. The resulting sheep was a new hardy merino that produced wool to equal the finest anywhere.

Others soon emulated Macarthur, and before long the strip of land between the coast of New South Wales and the Blue Mountains, a range that until now had proved an impenetrable barrier to the hinterland, was filled to capacity; it was imperative to find new grazing land. When a route through the mountains was finally found between 1813 and 1815, the fertile river plains beyond were opened up, and sheep farming rapidly spread; by 1849 there were 16 million sheep in Australia, by the turn of the century 100 million. Today, over 80 per cent of sheep in Australia are merinos—an enduring tribute to Macarthur's vision.

◀ Convicts carry heavy loads of stone for the first road through the Blue Mountains.

Sheep farming rapidly spread as more and more prime pasture land like this was discovered. ▶

with flocks and herds were flooding into one of the great pasture areas of the world. This breakthrough, as Blaxland put it, 'changed the aspect of the colony from a confined insulated tract of land to a rich extensive continent'.

It would, however, be wrong to imagine that as soon as the settlers crossed the divide they found themselves in a land of milk and honey. The Murray–Darling Basin beyond does indeed contain rich pastures; but it also contains swamp, scrubland and tracts of poor red soil. It is subjected to long periods of drought, punctuated by short spasms of violent flooding. And as one heads west the terrain becomes more and more arid as it merges into the heart of the continent, the outback.

Exploring the Outback from the South

The outback is very dry—most parts of it have less than six inches of rain a year; it is very hot—in many places the average midday temperature is over 90°F; it is greened by few oases, is crossed by no trade routes, and is the second only to the Sahara as the largest area of desert and semidesert in the world.

By the middle of the 19th century the whaling industry was in sharp decline, and wool was the mainstay of Australia's economy. John Macarthur, a lieutenant with the second convict fleet, bought South African merinos in the 1790s to crossbreed with hardier stock, and the number of sheep in the continent trebled in a decade, making Australia one of the largest wool producers in the world. Among the first people to seek new pastures in the outback, and in particular to seek the Great Inland Sea which in those days was thought to lie in the centre of the continent, was Charles Sturt.

Between 1828 and 1845 Sturt explored the southeast interior. On his final expedition in 1844 he set out with 4 wagons, 11 horses, 15 men and, optimistically, a boat. His diary paints a vivid picture of his trials and tribulations: 'The natives say "if you go farther your wagons will tip over and you will die. For there is no great sea in the heart of the desert, nor water nor grass nor a stick to light a fire with"…All around us we have a boundless expanse without a landmark to guide us. The temperature stands at 118°[F] in the shade, our instruments have split, our hair has ceased to grow, scurvy afflicts us. This morning Mr. Poole [the expedition surveyor] died…Nothing could exceed the sterile character of this terrible desert…The moon being full we continued our journey, at times across the dry white bed of salt lagoons, at times along the top of sandy ridges. The sky is cloudy, but no rain ever falls. We are struggling against difficulties that can not be overcome by human perseverance.'

Sturt pushed to within 150 miles of the centre of the continent, and then very wisely turned back. As the Royal Geographical Society pointed out when they gave him their gold medal, the difference between a great explorer and a dead one is that the former knows when to give up.

Exploring the Outback from the North

In the northeast, the outback merges into heavily wooded wetland, saturated each year by violent thunderstorms and monsoon rains. First to cross this remote area, in 1844, was the German-born explorer Ludwig Leichhardt (who inspired *Voss*, the novel by Australian Nobel laureate Patrick White). Financed by businessmen anxious to find new pastures, Leichhardt was an unlikely explorer. Striding ahead of his ill-assorted, poorly organised team, brandishing a Prussian officer's sword, he seemed to court disaster yet managed somehow to achieve success. His route from Jimbour Station, near today's Brisbane, took him first through Queensland's Mackenzie table-land, which he described as 'fine country, well adapted for pastoral purposes', then through more difficult terrain around the Gulf of Carpentaria, where he became bogged down and was attacked by Aborigines. Undaunted, he struggled on to Port Essington (near present-day Darwin) after a journey of nearly 15 months and 3,000 miles. A few years later he set out to cross the continent from east to west. He was never heard of again.

Augustus Gregory was one of four brothers, all competent surveyors. In 1855, he led an expedition financed by the British government, opening up new grazing land along Leichhardt's original route. In 1858 he journeyed from Brisbane to Adelaide, finding a route between Lake Frome and Lake Torrens.

At the same time as explorers such as these were probing at the edge of the outback, others were heading into its centre or attempting to traverse it from coast to coast. Among the former were John McDouall Stuart, who in 1860 became the first non-Aborigine to reach the geographical centre of the continent, and William Gosse, who in 1873 became the first non-Aborigine to climb the great sacred monolith of Uluru (Ayers Rock). Among the latter were the luckless Burke and Wills whose epic journey is retraced in the second part of this book.

Aladdin's Cave

As long ago as 1846 one of the Gregory brothers wrote of west Australia: 'This land is extremely dry, with immense salt marshes and sandstone cliffs... iron pyrites and plumbago found in the gneiss indicate a metaliferous formation, and I have little doubt

▲ Rainwater, washing over Uluru for millions of years, has slowly worn gullies and hollows into its flanks.

The near-vertical slopes of Uluru are accentuated by its striped appearance, resulting from the sandwiching together of layers of rock. ▼

The Giant Island Rock of Uluru

T HE EXPLORER WILLIAM GOSSE said of it in 1873: 'This
rock is certainly the most wonderful natural feature
I have ever seen'. He was referring to one of the biggest
rocks in the world—Ayers Rock, as he named it, or
Uluru, its preferred Aboriginal name.

Sculpted by the elements and transformed into
myriad hues by the sun, Uluru is one of Australia's most
enduring wonders. It soars to 1,142 feet above the
surrounding plain, and is six miles in circumference.
It stands alone, a potent symbol of the outback. For the
Aborigines Uluru is a sacred site visibly scarred by the
battles of their ancestors from the Dreamtime, the
legendary beginning of the world. The rock's strange
shapes are their ancestors' bodies; water stains on its
flanks mark the points where their blood flowed. The
descendants of the Dreamtime heroes have made their
own marks on the surface of this monument with
paintings and carvings, many of which are thousands
of years old.

But according to scientists Uluru is much older than
the Aboriginal culture that has revered it for so long.
They also tell us that it is not just an isolated rock but
the top of a huge buried hill that was once one of many
hills on the now flat landscape. Between 140 and 120
million years ago a great sea swept into central
Australia, and Uluru became an island; waves pounded
at its base to form the caves now so sacred to the
Aborigines. When the sea finally receded, Uluru was
left as an island again—this time in a sea of sand.

**An Aborigine contemplates life in one of Uluru's caves.
His people became the rock's legal owners in 1985.** ▶

▲ **Rising red and majestic
above the plain, Uluru,
sacred site of the Aborigines,
dominates the landscape as
far as the eye can see.**

**Aboriginal paintings adorn
Uluru's caves. Many are
ancient, but are regularly
retouched to revive their
symbolic powers.** ▶

that a further search would reveal sources of mineral wealth.' He was proved right. During the 19th century Australia was at different times the world's largest producer of gold, silver, copper, tin, lead and coal.

Discoveries in New South Wales and Victoria in 1851 revealed one of the richest, most easily worked goldfields in the world. Soon nearly 2,000 prospectors a week were flocking into Melbourne, paying a £1-per-week licence fee and disappearing west into the rolling hills where the Great Divide tapers off into the Grampians. A few made fortunes; but the real beneficiary of the gold rushes was the colony of Victoria. Melbourne became a financial centre and the gold rushes set off what has been a recurring theme in Australian history: the periodic influx of large numbers of energetic people from the outside world. In 1852, a round total of 95,000 new immigrants arrived in New South Wales and Victoria. Some may have been drifters, law-breakers and misfits, but most were active, intelligent people eager to 'have a go' at making their fortune. They included skilled artisans, professional men like engineers and doctors, and academics with university degrees; and they brought new ideas and new blood. In their wake came hangers-on as diverse as the Chinese market gardeners who fed them, the dance-hall girls who entertained them and the Irish fiddlers whose camp-fire ballads have become part of Australian folklore.

During the early 20th century most of Australia's wealth stemmed from farming. It was only with the outbreak of the Second World War that the treasures of the outback were exploited on a massive scale, with vast tracts of land being ripped up to extract some of the world's most extensive deposits of aluminium, silver, lead, copper, zinc and uranium.

Many States: One Nation

Australia has been one nation for less than 100 years, the Commonwealth of Australia being officially declared on January 1, 1901. What had been separate colonies then became states. The Australian Capital Territory (around Canberra) and the Northern Territory, both administered directly by the national government, were set up in 1911. The constitution gave only limited powers to the central government; a lot of power was left in the hands of the states; and to prevent the large and populous states (like Victoria) riding roughshod over the small and sparsely populated states (like Tasmania) each was given the same number of representatives in the senate. This has helped the six states (Queensland, New South Wales, Victoria, Tasmania, South Australia, Western Australia) and

▲ Inside an opal miner's cave at Coober Pedy. Searing heat outside makes such housing a sensible option.

The cones of debris from opal-mine shafts create a surreal, lunar landscape. The prize: iridescent opals glowing within the rock (*inset*). ▶

The characteristic red stain betrays this site's use as a loading wharf for bauxite, one of Australia's principal exports. ▼

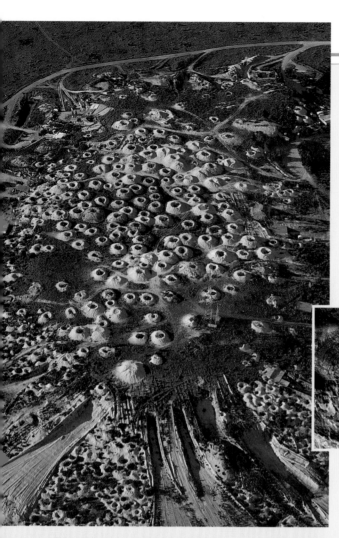

Australia's Buried Treasure

A**S ONE NEWSPAPER REPORTER** put it: 'A complete mental madness appears to have seized every member of the community.' He was referring not to some virulent epidemic, but to the gold fever that gripped Bathurst, New South Wales, when gold was discovered there in 1851. Just a few months later more gold was found at Ballarat in Victoria. Immigrants flocked to Australia to seek their fortunes; in only 10 years the country's population had trebled.

These days gold is just one of any number of minerals mined in resource-rich Australia. The country is one of the world's leading producers of diamonds, coal and iron ore, and by the late 1980s was *the* leading producer of bauxite, the principal ore of aluminium. Nearly 100,000 people in Australia are employed in the mining industry, and its activities occupy tens of thousands of acres of land. Yet one part of the industry has remained free from such massive development, despite being a world leader: opal mining. At Coober Pedy in South Australia, the country's principal opal-mining site, the labour-intensive extraction has proved uneconomical for big companies. Instead, individual miners form partnerships with up to three others, each working an area of roughly 50 square yards. The opals are extracted from galleries hollowed out at the bottom of narrow shafts, each new shaft leaving a telltale cone of rubble at its entrance. Many miners rarely see the light of day, for in order to escape the scorching summer temperatures they live in cave-houses hewn from the same rocks as the opals.

▲ **Despite the development of modern mining techniques, there are still those who seek gold the traditional way. This individual looks as though he has struck lucky!**

▲ Traditional ways can harmonise with the modern world: bark paintings like this one are now highly prized in the art world.

The Yarrabah Mission in Queensland is one of many that provide necessities for those Aborigines who have lost their old lifestyle but who have not become integrated into modern Australia. ▶

Ancient Australians in a Modern World

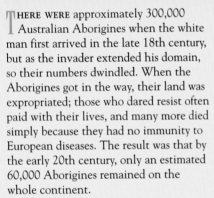

THERE WERE approximately 300,000 Australian Aborigines when the white man first arrived in the late 18th century, but as the invader extended his domain, so their numbers dwindled. When the Aborigines got in the way, their land was expropriated; those who dared resist often paid with their lives, and many more died simply because they had no immunity to European diseases. The result was that by the early 20th century, only an estimated 60,000 Aborigines remained on the whole continent.

Then, in the mid-20th century, Aborigines became increasingly vocal about their plight; many white Australians, too, began to pressurise the authorities to grant their compatriots equal rights. Finally, in 1967, Aborigines were given the vote; there were high hopes that they would become fully integrated into modern Australia.

But integration was not the whole answer. Many Aborigines wanted to continue their traditional ways on their tribal land, with which they held profound spiritual ties. In 1982 a group led by a man called Eddie Mabo (of Torres Strait Islander descent) brought a test case against the Queensland state government to claim back their land. After 10 long years, the courts ruled in

favour of Mabo, making it easier for Aborigines to gain title to their traditional lands all over Australia.

The Mabo ruling did not solve all the problems facing today's Aborigines. Many, having lost touch with their old ways, have found nothing to replace them with—unemployment among Aborigines is at least three times the national average; some, without jobs,

homes or land, rely on the government or on missions to provide their basic needs. But many Aborigines now feel they have choices about how to live: they can either embrace the new Australia— like the athlete Cathy Freeman, who has represented her country in the international sporting arena—or keep up at least some of their traditions, living at one with their land, as in the past.

Athlete Cathy Freeman was named Young Australian of the Year in 1990. Her sporting success is evidence of increasing choice for Aborigines today.

Making headdresses and practising the didgeridoo are important preparations for a corroboree, or tribal festival. Aborigines have had to fight for the right to live like this on their land.

the two nationally administered territories to retain their individuality, often epitomised by their own brands of beer and until comparatively recently their own gauges of railway; but it has also made it difficult for the national government to enforce legislation on key issues like environmental protection.

Immediately after federation Australia was still very much an outpost of the British way of life. Ties with Britain were strengthened by two world wars, during which thousands of Australians gave their lives as far from home as the Dardanelles and the sands of Libya to help a country most had never seen. However, towards the end of the Second World War many Australians noticed that in their hour of need they were saved from the Japanese more by the efforts of the Americans than of the British; and since then Australia has increasingly loosened ties with its 'mother' country (there is talk of becoming a republic) and strengthened ties with its Pacific neighbours.

One result has been the influx of large numbers of non-British immigrants. After the Second World War the Australian government anxiously compared the overcrowded islands of Indonesia and Japan with its own sparsely populated territory, and coined the catchphrase, 'Populate or perish'. Non-British migrants were invited to settle, and soon people from southern Europe were pouring into Australia at the rate of nearly 100,000 a year; within a decade Melbourne had become the second largest Greek-speaking city in the world. A generation later Australia opened its doors to Southeast Asian refugees. This marked the end of the White Australia policy which had been introduced in the early 1900s. Today, more than one quarter of Australia's population was born overseas.

One reason why these postwar immigrants enriched Australian life and fitted in well is that Australia has much to offer them—not least freedom. Another reason is that the immigrants themselves have tended to be adaptable—those who quit their family and their job in, say, Greece or Vietnam are likely to be more adventurous and receptive to new ideas than those left behind. Which perhaps explains why if you ask a European nowadays for a decision he is likely to say, 'I'll sleep on it', whereas an Australian is likely to say, 'I'll give it a go'.

Aboriginal Rights and Wrongs

Before white people ever saw Australia, the Aborigines had been living there for thousands of years. Yet when white settlers came, the British government declared the continent 'terra nullius', or unoccupied. This meant that the Europeans could take possession of any land they wanted, and in many

The Impact of the New: Threats to the Environment

THE AUSTRALIAN ENVIRONMENT has undergone more changes in the last 200 years than at any time since the Aborigines first came to the continent at least 45,000 years ago. Although the Aborigines had an undeniable impact on the land in which they lived—for example, they deliberately set bushfires to control growth and to drive out animals—their simple lifestyle fitted in with the natural order. What is more, Aborigines had great respect for their environment, believing as they did that their ancestors actually formed part of it.

The European settlers, however, coming from the newly industrial West, had an entirely different outlook, one based on using the environment to their own ends. They soon set about clearing forests and woodland to make room for settlements and farming. Although much of Australia's remaining rain forest is now protected in national parks, clearing is still practised.

When abundant mineral resources were found in Australia in the 19th century, mining began in earnest, and soon became a major source of revenue for the national economy. In some areas mining companies have managed to make their operations very unobtrusive, but in others open-cast mining has laid waste vast tracts of land; once mining in a particular area has ceased, the land can take decades to recover.

Sometimes, however, humans are only indirectly to blame for damage to the Australian environment. A combination of factors led to the extinction in southeast Australia of the Tasmanian bettong, a small marsupial which is now found only in Tasmania. Much of the grassland on which it lived was turned over to farming, and two species of animal that came to Australia with the settlers hastened its demise: the rabbit, which overgrazed its remaining habitat, and the fox, which preyed on it. Another introduced animal that has upset Nature's balance is the water buffalo, whose grazing and wallowing has polluted waterholes and mangrove swamps fringing the Gulf of Carpentaria.

Tasmanian bettongs—small nocturnal marsupials—were once found in mainland Australia, but foxes helped drive them to extinction there, and they now survive only in fox-free Tasmania.

Vehicles at the bottom of this open-cast gold mine at Mount Magnet in Western Australia are dwarfed by the gigantic hole the mine has created; the landscape will take decades to recover.

European settlers practised widespread deforestation, and the practice continues today. Deforestation not only destroys wildlife habitats, but also encourages soil erosion and interferes with local climates.

Water buffalo were introduced for their meat and hide, but they have turned wild, damaging waterholes and swamp habitats. Recapture and culling are two methods of control, but neither can solve the problem completely.

cases Aborigines were dispossessed with great cruelty. An oral history published in Australia recounts how a newly established cattle station was visited by a group of the Djumindjung tribe; they were hungry, and 'not knowing the white men's horses were sacred', killed one and ate it. The angry station-owner cooked a bowl of rice and invited the men, women and children to eat. But the rice had been laced with arsenic. When the Aborigines realised they had been poisoned, they rushed to the nearest waterhole and tried to eat mud to make them spew up the poison. As they writhed about in the water, the station-owner and his foreman shot them. This was not an isolated incident. In several parts of Australia, (Tasmania, for example), whole groups were exterminated.

The Aborigines who survived were unable to own property or get many types of work; while many children of mixed marriages were forcibly taken from their parents and brought up in foster homes. After the Second World War, assimilation became the order of the day and large numbers had to leave their tribal lands and live in towns, often on the fringes of the settlement, dependent upon welfare for housing and other necessities. Only in the last few decades has government policy focused on helping Aborigines to rebuild their traditional ties with the land, encouraging them to take over the management of longstanding Aboriginal reserves or giving them control of increasing areas of former Crown land.

This is being hastened by a legal judgment known as the Mabo Ruling. In 1992 the High Court ruled that Australia was not *terra nullius* at the time of European colonisation and that where Aborigines could prove a continuous association with Crown land, they could claim legal title to it. In addition, in recent years some National Parks, including Uluru, have been handed back by the government to their traditional owners.

Safeguarding a Unique Heritage

For its non-Aborigine inhabitants Australia is still seen as a new country, but in much the same way as its oldest inhabitants, non-Aborigines are proud of the country's idiosyncratic flora and fauna, and the unspoilt nature of its terrain. So it is no surprise that many Australians today are conservationists, determined to safeguard unique assets such as the World Heritage Areas of the Great Barrier Reef and Kakadu National Park.

The Great Barrier Reef is amazing not only for its size and complexity, but also for the cornucopia of life that it supports. Stretching for 1,250 miles along the coast of Queensland, it covers an area almost twice the size of England, and consists of a mosaic of jewel-like islands, and barrier, platform and fringe reefs all fashioned out of the skeletons of tiny creatures called coral polyps. There are roughly 3,000 of these individual islands and reefs, and together they form the showcase for a spectacular underwater world. A square kilometre of reefwater contains more animal life than the same area anywhere else on Earth. It was the invention of the aqualung which opened the eyes of ordinary people to the wonders of this beautiful underwater world, and in the early 1960s a committee was formed to protect the reef. The result was the creation first of a marine park of limited extent, then in 1981 of a World Heritage Area, which today includes virtually all the reefs and islands between Torres Strait and the Tropic of Capricorn.

Today most who visit the outback feel as though they are very small individuals in a very large, very ancient land. And this is particularly the case in another World Heritage Area, Kakadu National Park, located in the heart of Arnhem Land, Northern Territory. For as one looks out over its harshly beautiful terrain, which seems to live and breathe to the recurring cycle of the wet and dry seasons, one has the feeling that this is the Earth as it was on some infinitely distant yesterday and still will be on some equally distant tomorrow.

The outback will never be tamed. Like the kangaroos and the gum trees, the red sands and the often-shining sun, it is part of Australia's heritage.

Introducing 'An Australian Challenge'

This was the vast and forbidding land into which Burke and Wills ventured in 1860. In those days no one had ever crossed the continent from south to north, and Burke was determined to be the first. He set out from Melbourne in command of a well-equipped expedition. From a base near Cooper Creek, four men set off for the Gulf of Carpentaria. They made it. But three of them died on the way back.

Posterity has placed the blame on the shoulders of the flamboyant Burke, who, it has been said, took undue risks and failed to get the best out of his camels. Tom Bergin wondered if this was fair. As curator of mammals at a zoo, Tom knew about camels; so he teamed up with three men who knew about the outback, and they set out with seven camels to retrace Burke's epic journey. This is their story. And when you have finished it, you may wonder not that Burke and Wills failed but that they came as close to success as they did.

▲ The reef acts as a magnet to tourists. The popular pastime of reef walking is now restricted to designated areas to protect the delicate corals.

Beautiful but deadly, the crown-of-thorns starfish can grow to two feet across, and devours coral polyps at the rate of one square yard a week. ▶

There seems to be no limit to the variety and colour of reef life. Here, fish and coral combine to cover just about every colour in the spectrum. ▼

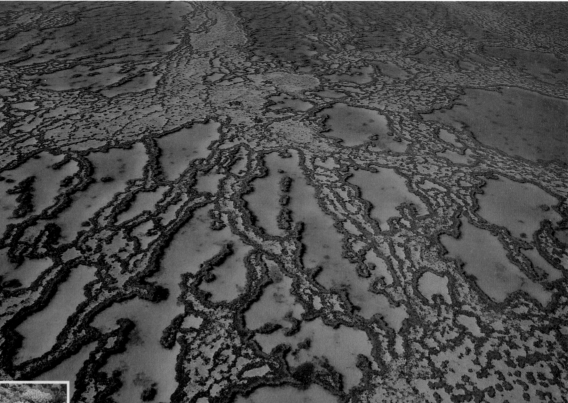

▲ The Great Barrier Reef, a delicate tracery of coral reefs and islands stretching along the eastern coast of Queensland, is the largest structure in the world made by living organisms.

The Great Barrier Reef: Conservation in Action

THE GREAT BARRIER REEF is one of the great natural wonders of the world, a spectacular formation of coral reefs and islands stretching over 1,250 miles along the eastern coast of Queensland. To gaze into these waters is to gaze upon the greatest concentration of animal life in the world. Death, too, is omnipresent here, for the coral itself is formed from millions of skeletons: a tiny anemone-like animal called a polyp manufactures a protective exterior skeleton, and when the polyp dies, it leaves the skeleton behind; as new polyps settle on the old ones and develop skeletons of their own, so the coral grows to form reefs.

But as effectively as these reefs, with their hard, jagged edges, repel all but the most intrepid sailors, so too they act like a magnet to tourists, whose activities can be very harmful: for example, every piece of coral broken off to decorate someone's mantel-piece will take years, even decades, to grow back. Added to such problems is chemical pollution in the sea, which damages reef life, and the fact that the petrochemical industry would love to exploit the oil that lies beneath the reef. There is even a natural threat in the form of the crown-of-thorns starfish, which eats coral polyps; some environmentalists, though, see Man's actions behind even this problem, blaming the creature's recent population explosion on overfishing of its natural predators.

Fortunately many of these threats have diminished since the Great Barrier Reef was made a World Heritage Area in 1981, with strict regulations governing the types of activities that can be practised there. Furthermore, constant monitoring of the reefs helps conservationists identify problems and take the necessary action to deal with them.

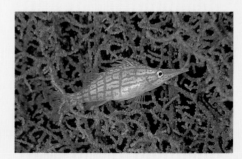

▲ One of the prettiest of the reef's 1,500 species of fish is the long-nosed hawkfish.

AN AUSTRALIAN CHALLENGE

by **Tom Bergin**

A condensation based on his book IN THE STEPS OF BURKE AND WILLS

Prologue

▲ Robert O'Hara Burke, leader of the expedition charged with finding a route across Australia.

▲ William Wills became Burke's second-in-command soon after the start of the expedition. He remained loyal to his leader to the very end.

THIS WAS TO BE the most lavishly equipped expedition in Australian history. The year was 1860, and although trade was expanding around the coast of the vast continent, there were still no overland routes between the British colonies in the south and the uncharted north. Communications and trade between Britain and Australia had, up to 1860, been by sail via Cape Horn or the Cape of Good Hope, and across to southern Australia on the Roaring Forties winds. However, with the opening of a shorter route via the Suez Canal and the introduction of steamships, the north coast of Australia would become the continent's closest point to Britain; overland trade routes to new northern ports were therefore seen as vital to the future of the southern cities. The southern Australian colony of Victoria, especially, saw that great advantages could be gained from the establishment of secure trading posts across the 1,500-mile wilderness between itself and the north coast. Nine thousand pounds—an enormous sum at the time—were raised in the colony's capital, Melbourne, to finance an expedition with the purpose of discovering a suitable route to the closest point on the north coast, the Gulf of Carpentaria. At its head rode Robert O'Hara Burke, whose choice as leader had aroused some comment in the colony: a cavalry officer of Irish birth, he was a brave but difficult man with a reputation for indecisiveness. Second-in-charge was George Landells, a self-styled 'camel expert'. The expedition also included William Wills, a quiet young Devonshire surveyor; John King, a soldier; Herman Beckler, a doctor; and Ludwig Becker, an artist; as well as a foreman, nine general hands and three Pathan camel drivers.

The expedition set out at the end of the Australian winter, on August 19, 1860. Eighteen men rode with Burke, and they took a huge amount of stores and equipment, carried in carts and on camels and horses. Burke was obviously not an easy man to be with, though, and by the time the expedition reached Menindee, 400 miles north of Melbourne, rifts had occurred within the party. Most notably Landells, the second-in-command, had resigned, as had Dr Beckler.

King was then put in charge of camels, and William Wills was promoted to second-in-command; also Burke took on new men, including 'Charley' (George) Gray, a sailor-turned-bushman he had met on the way.

At Menindee Burke had to spell (rest) the stock for three weeks and reconsider his whole mode of progress. Ahead the country was largely unknown and on the experience of the last five weeks there was no guarantee that the expedition's cumbersome carts would get through. If he loaded the stores and equipment onto the horses and camels he would be able to travel faster. But with all his beasts fully loaded, he could still only carry five tons odd—a quarter of the remaining stores. And he had nowhere near enough packsaddles, so his carrying capacity was reduced to about half of that. Furthermore, the locals warned him that the few waterholes to the north were drying up fast. Burke could either make a dash for Cooper Creek—some 400 miles to the north—with provisions for six months or so, or wait several months at Menindee until the next good season and in the meantime reorganise his team.

But another factor had entered the equation. Victoria was not the only colony to see the potential of links with the north. The South Australian government had offered a reward to the first man to cross the continent from south to north. Five months earlier a similar expedition, led by John McDouall Stuart, had set out from Adelaide. Stuart had been forced by the arduous conditions to turn back, but on hearing that Burke's expedition was underway planned an immediate follow-up. News of Stuart's second attempt reached Burke just a few weeks into his journey, and the dashing Irish officer determined to beat the cautious Scot. It was to be a race.

If Burke waited until the next good rains, Stuart would win, and the citizens of Victoria would be most unimpressed to hear that their widely publicised expedition had been halted only a few weeks' ride north of Melbourne. He decided to go, leaving a depot of stores at Menindee to be brought up later. Several of his stock were not fit to travel, and these he would have to leave behind, as well as those without saddles. He also cut his men back, leaving Dr Beckler in charge—he had already resigned, but agreed to stay on and look after the depot.

On October 19, 1860, Burke left Menindee for Cooper Creek with eight men, fifteen horses, sixteen camels and six months' supply of stores. By chance, he had encountered a man who knew this country, one William Wright, who agreed to guide them as far as the Torowoto Swamp far to the north. Guide them he did: they made it safely across 200 miles of plain in ten days.

◀ The original full expedition team, painted here by one of its members, Ludwig Becker, was quite a cavalcade, carrying supplies for almost any eventuality. Burke soon realised he could never make it with all this luggage and jettisoned much of it at Menindee.

A contemporay painting by Nicholas Chevalier of Burke, Wills and King limping towards Cooper Creek. One of the hungry camels reaches longingly towards a rare morsel. ▶

During the time Wright spent with the expedition, Burke must have been impressed by the man and his bushmanship for he offered him the position of third officer of the expedition provided that the Melbourne committee had not already appointed someone to replace Landells. Wright accepted the offer and, having arranged for Aboriginal guides to take the expedition on to Cooper Creek, he and his two trackers returned to Menindee. His task: to assemble a relief team and bring the remainder of the stores up to Cooper Creek. Burke had told him he would probably send back a team of pack animals to help convey the stores up. This was a crucial mistake: there is no room for 'probably' or 'maybe' in that country.

Thirteen days after Wright returned to Menindee, Burke struck Cooper Creek but, following some incidents with the Aborigines there, he appears to have decided that he could not spare any of the men to take the pack-team back.

Burke left four men at Cooper Creek to establish a further supply base, with William Brahe, a well-educated young Prussian, in charge. Burke himself, with only three others—William Wills, Charley Gray and John King—went on with one horse and six camels, carrying barely enough supplies for a three-month dash to the coast and back.

It was a rash enterprise. Burke had chosen to travel in summer—the rainy season in the north—in order to be sure of drinking water *en route*, but he had taken no account of the mud and floods he would encounter. Impenetrable swamps near the coast prevented his party from ever quite reaching the sea. When Burke decided to turn back he had already left it too late. Meanwhile,

Wright, who had given up waiting at Menindee for Burke's promised pack animals, had set off regardless with a relief expedition. But he was still a long way south of Cooper Creek.

Burke and his companions were weak and ill, and Burke was forced to kill and butcher one of his camels during a break in the rain. Charley Gray, however, continued to decline and, after two more weeks, he died. The other three pressed on. Conditions on the journey back to the depot at Cooper Creek were appalling and the three months Burke had set himself were long exceeded.

At Cooper Creek Brahe was waiting impatiently both for Wright to come up from Menindee and for Burke to return from the north. Eventually Brahe decided he could wait no longer. His party was suffering badly from scurvy, and Burke had said: 'If I am not back in three months, you may consider me perished.' He had also at various times suggested that he might be picked up by ship or return by way of Queensland.

Brahe buried emergency food supplies under a coolabah tree, in case Burke should make it back that way, with a sign carved on the tree instructing him to dig. Then Brahe and his men rode away.

That same day, only nine hours later, Burke, Wills and King arrived at the coolabah tree. The fire was still warm.

They read Brahe's sign, dug, and found the food. But they were by now desperately sick and they needed medical supplies—of which there were none—far more than food. Burke decided that it was useless to try to catch Brahe, and that his best chance was to follow the creek west to Mount Hopeless and then head south till they found a cattle property in South Australia; his two surviving camels could carry the stores they had dug up at the Dig Tree (as the infamous coolabah became known). They buried their journals in the Dig Tree cache, with a note detailing their plans, and covered the cache up as they had found it, before slowly heading west. Meanwhile, Brahe's party had met up with Wright at Bulloo, less than 150 miles away to the southeast. Wright had had just as difficult a time of it as the exploring party up north. Brahe and Wright rode back to the Dig Tree. Seeing the cache apparently undisturbed, they finally gave Burke up for dead and returned to their own sick and dying.

Burke and Wills both died some weeks later. We know of their fate only because King, the sole survivor, lived to tell the tale. He was found at the point of death by Aborigines and eventually made it back to civilisation after a rescue party tracked him down.

The tragic story of Burke and Wills is part of the folk history of Australia. Historians have long argued over the reasons for Burke's failure to reach the coast, and over the misunderstandings that led to the deaths of all but one of his party. Burke was a brave man, but inexperienced.

Was he a good leader? Was he wrong to travel in summer? Was it his use of camels that brought him to disaster? Or was he simply too impetuous? ▪

▲ This document, signed by Wills and describing the appalling predicament he and his companions found themselves in, was left in the Dig Tree cache, but tragically Brahe and Wright failed to find it. A few weeks later, Wills and Burke were dead.

CHAPTER 1

The First Step

BURKE AND WILLS HAD BEEN ON MY MIND FOR SOME TIME before I decided to retrace their steps and try to set the record straight. I think it happened gradually; minor irritation slowly turned to anger as I read one armchair critic after another pontificating on the mistakes of the expedition.

The Royal Commission of Enquiry set up after the expedition in 1861 cast the blame upon Burke and his officers without having the slightest knowledge of camels or deserts, of hunger or scurvy. It almost seemed as if the facts were irrelevant so long as they had scapegoats to give to the colony's angry public. Surely, however, one cannot apportion blame until all the facts are available, and, more than that, one must understand the facts to interpret their significance.

Subsequent writers had done little more than echo the Commission's findings, branding Burke a fool, Brahe a deserter and Wright a dithering incompetent. Personally, I was convinced that the major cause of the disaster which befell Burke was the timing of his expedition to the Gulf of Carpentaria. He left Cooper Creek at the height of summer, subjecting his men and beasts to the intense heat of the central deserts and then to the mud, rain and stupefying humidity of the monsoon season in the tropical north.

I was Curator of Mammals at Sydney's Taronga Zoo, and I reckoned I knew quite a bit about camels. Camels have feet like soup plates, perfect for walking on sand

▲ This Himalayan tahr— a type of wild goat—at Taronga Zoo looks quite blasé about the fact that it has one of the best views in Sydney, overlooking the famous opera house.

but almost impossible to pull out of mud. Once the soup plate is covered with a foot of mud, the camel is virtually immobilised.

Perhaps Burke was blinded by camels' ability to survive without water. Earlier explorers with horses, and often sheep and cattle, had relied on finding water as they went along. They used scouts, either Aborigines or experienced white bushmen, to go ahead and map out a route from waterhole to waterhole. These scouts would then wait for the main party to catch up and pass the time by fishing or hunting, thus supplementing the dried provisions.

◀ Camel racing has recently been a highlight of Sydney's annual Royal Easter Show. Some of these competitors have entered into the spirit of the occasion by donning Middle Eastern style headdresses.

Burke, however, believed that with camels he could set out on a compass bearing with no need of Aboriginal guides to find water for him, or to catch the odd fish. However, he, his three companions and the horses needed water, and the camels would have to carry it. I felt that had Burke used Aboriginal guides he would have had no need to carry water, and would have had access to useful edible plants and animals into the bargain. If he had made the journey in winter, I also reasoned, he would have been able to get to the Gulf and back on the three months' provisions that his pack animals could carry.

All this was, of course, just a theory like all the others, and, almost 120 years after the original expedition, it was likely to remain so. Still, I used to sit and ruminate on it all in odd quiet moments, just one more armchair expert developing his own biased theories.

Then I met Greg McHugh. He strode into my office one day, a total stranger, sat himself down and without further ado asked: 'Do you want to buy camels?'

I have to admit that my office was less than glamorous. Located in a disused women's toilet block in the zoo grounds, it was wedged in between a hyena cage and a Bengal tiger. Even so, my visitor had come to the right place, for I had an infertile camel herd on my hands and was actively looking for good breeding camels to buy.

Greg was tall and rangy with a dark mane beneath his battered hat and a beard brushing his chest. His skin was burned to leather and ingrained with the red dust of the deserts, but his daunting appearance was offset by twinkling eyes and a wide friendly grin. He was a camel trader from out west, who was down in the 'big smoke' for the camel races at the Royal Easter Show. (Once superseded by cars and trucks, camels were at first left to run in the wild. Today, however, they are being caught and tamed again for racing and for tourist trips.)

A deal was quickly struck, and as we yarned on about camels and prices I raised the question of Burke's dash to the Gulf. 'You know,' he said, 'it's funny you should mention that because it's always fascinated me.'

A map showing the routes of Burke and Wills and of the author. ▼

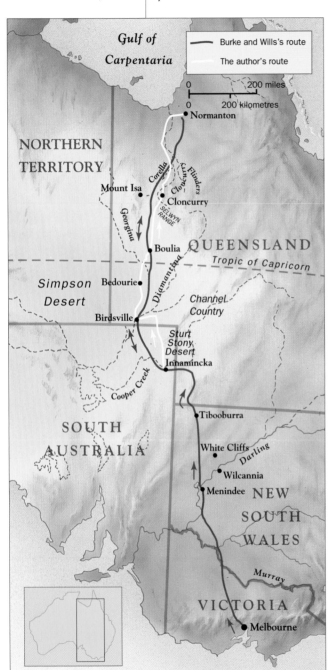

That night after dinner we started sifting through the evidence, assessing each of Burke's decisions in the light of Greg's experience. Greg had made many long trips by camel, horse and donkey, and had a pretty good idea of just how hard each type of beast could be pushed. He had recently gathered a large number of wild donkeys and camels in the Northern Territory and had walked them by stages to Gulgong via Broken Hill, a distance of some 1,600 miles. His comments tended to confirm my theories. Pack camels, if pushed, could cover more than thirty miles a day and Greg had used them on sustained treks. Thus Burke's dash was not particularly foolhardy: provided the camels did not strike mud it was feasible to go from Cooper Creek to the Gulf and back in twelve weeks. 'In fact,' Greg said offhandedly, 'if a bloke did it in winter, it shouldn't be all that bad a trip.'

I looked up from my book-strewn desk and we stared at each other for a moment. A huge grin spread across his face. 'Why not give it a go?' he said.

I thought for a minute. Apart from finding out exactly what problems arise with camels on such a trip, it would be a unique opportunity to see the country, and would certainly be the best way to test our theory. 'Why not?' I replied.

With his practical turn of mind, Greg offered a refreshing insight into the use of camels for exploration, one which complemented my somewhat academic approach. (I held degrees in biology and veterinary medicine and was studying history at night.) Together we worked out a way to test our theory. We would attempt to follow the trail Burke and Wills had blazed, using camels just as they had done, but at a different time of year—the three months of the dry northern winter. That way we could prove if the season made the journey possible in just twelve weeks. Furthermore, historians argued about the exact route Burke took: if I compared the terrain described in Wills's diaries with my own observations during my journey, I might be able to settle that point too.

The Team Gathers

Inevitably our expedition was dogged by setbacks. Initially there was a sudden withdrawal of financial backing, which we managed to overcome, and then massive floods occurred out west, which we waited out. Leukaemia, however, was a setback we could neither overcome nor wait out. When tragically it struck Greg down, with our expedition scarcely out of the planning stage, I was prepared to see the entire project abandoned. Not Greg, though.

He had entered into the preparations for the trip with tireless enthusiasm, and was never the type to let anything upset him; he simply arranged for his brother, Paddy, to go in his place, and continued to take part in setting up the expedition from his hospital bed. We were not to let his death prevent the trip, he kept insisting: 'Go while the season lasts.'

Paddy and I had met only a few times but, although he lacked Greg's experience, he had handled camels. In fact, like many bushmen, he had done quite a number of things: plumbing, fencing, even parachuting! At present he was breaking in a few of the camels Greg had selected for the trip.

▲ The author, whose plan was to retrace Burke and Wills's steps to find out why they failed.

It was a bleak wintry day when they buried Greg. By then there was no question of abandoning the expedition he had worked so hard to bring about. Most of its equipment was already gathered in Sydney. One of the few remaining problems was locating the two men Paddy and I hoped would accompany us, Nugget Gnalkenga and his son Frankie.

Nugget was an old friend of Greg's who had ridden with him on his long trek in the Northern Territory and so had experienced the type of journey we were about to undertake. He was an elder of the Pitjantjatjara people, from the sand-dune desert country in the Petermann Ranges region of the Northern Territory; our last report of his and Frankie's whereabouts was some weeks old. When we finally made contact, at the Hermannsburg Mission in Central Australia, and they agreed to come, we were relieved and delighted. Now we would make up a team of four, the same as Burke's original team on their final dash to the Gulf. Already, though, we had one undeniable advantage over Burke: unlike him we would have two Aborigines with us—people of wisdom and good humour, with a storehouse of local knowledge and survival expertise no European could equal.

▲ Seasoned bushman Paddy McHugh, who replaced his brother Greg on the expedition when the latter tragically died.

Not long after Greg's funeral I loaded all the food, guns, torches, medical supplies and radio and navigational equipment—including a sextant and a computer—into a Land-Rover and, with a sad farewell to my long-suffering wife and two little girls, set out from our home in Sydney for Dubbo, an easy 200-mile drive northwest from Sydney. Dubbo is a prosperous town and the site of Taronga's overflow zoo. I knew it well and it was an ideal assembly point. There I was to meet up with the rest of the team, human and camel, before moving on by truck to the town of Wilcannia and then on again via Tibooburra to Cooper Creek.

My driver was an old friend, Dave Cody, the head mammal-keeper at Taronga Zoo, who was shortly to embark on his own adventure: to fly to England and bring back four African elephants—one, a bull—as deck freight on a cargo ship. We should have had plenty to talk about, but in fact the trip was almost silent. The enormity of the task ahead left me with a lot to think about and little in the way of friendly chatter.

Paddy and the camels were already in Dubbo when we arrived, and Nugget and Frankie came in soon afterwards, having flown across from Alice Springs. I took to them immediately. Nugget had that gnarled, serene look you see in old sea captains. With his shabby stetson hat pulled down low over woolly steel-grey hair and a black briar pipe protruding from a set of silver whiskers, he seemed to have mastered all the problems of life. He was soft-spoken and direct. He was happy to give his opinion when asked, but otherwise would just puff his pipe and inspect the horizon while the rest of us debated.

▲ Nugget Gnalkenga, an Aboriginal elder, would help the team survive the rigours of the desert.

His son Frankie was a slightly built lad, shy, with a smile like a grand piano. When I first met him he was rigged up in pullovers and a parka several sizes too large for him, above skinny jeans and an old pair of sandshoes without socks or laces. Although he was always ready to help, he was afraid of getting things wrong. If he was not given specific tasks he tended to lounge around, embarrassed, like many adolescents in the company of strange adults.

When all our bedrolls and provisions were gathered together and heaped up alongside the saddles and saddlebags, water tanks and harness, the pile looked awesome. We were soon hard at it, packing everything into the saddlebags and giving the camels some last-minute treatment—anti-ringworm ointment for one and some 'behavioural tuition' (smacks on the nose for biting) for another.

▲ For Nugget's shy teenage son, Frankie, the expedition would be a chance to learn desert lore from his father.

At this stage we had seven camels. Larrikin (Australian for 'rascal') was the biter, as rumbustious and basically likable as his name suggests. Paddymelon was the ringworm sufferer; a paddymelon (or 'pademelon') is a species of small forest kangaroo, and our Paddymelon had all its speed and nervousness. Walloper was big and galumphing, Ginger had reddish hair, Alice had come from Alice Springs, and Frances and Cleo were simply Frances and Cleo. This was all that we knew so far. Their very different natures would emerge in due course.

When at last everything seemed in order, checked and double-checked, we fed the camels and unrolled our swags around the fire. An Australian swag is a bedroll, a canvas bag usually containing a couple of blankets and a pillow stuffed with spare clothes. Tents were too heavy to carry. In the frosty winter's night, we did our best to get some sleep. When dawn came and we roused ourselves, dark areas on our pillows clearly marked the outline of our heads and hands where no frost had fallen.

We rubbed our frozen hands in front of the fire. 'I reckon this here's one problem we won't face in the desert, mate,' Paddy muttered, and I agreed with him. We were dead wrong.

The camels were desert bred and chosen for their stamina, not for their table manners. When the time came to leave for Wilcannia they refused point-blank to be loaded into the waiting truck, and it was all we could do, with the help of several hefty truck drivers, to drag them in, roaring steadily, inch by struggling inch. Once inside, each camel was 'hushed down' into a kneeling position, one which they could maintain for days quite comfortably, being equipped with horny pads on their knees and chests to take the weight.

The way they go down is one of the most awkward movements I have ever seen. It is even more awkward when you are riding the beast. On the order 'hush' the camel stops still and roars continuously while it looks around at the terrain—camels are understandably reluctant to hush down on stony or sloping ground. Having selected a spot, the animal first drops forward onto its knees, flinging you forward, then rocks abruptly back onto its haunches, flicking you back through a ninety-degree arc. Just when it seems that you are destined to dismount precipitously backwards over its rump, the camel lowers its forelegs and comes to rest on its elbows, at which point you rock forward, slightly dazed, back into your original position. When rising, the camel carries out the whole process in reverse order, but even more abruptly.

Camels do not have a ready willingness to rise or kneel on command; their only natural tendency is to bite and kick. Paddy—and Greg in his day—had spent many bruising hours in the stockyard trying to replace the latter vices with the former virtues. But on our first day they all seemed to have completely forgotten their training, which considerably delayed our departure from Dubbo.

Distances between towns in Australia can be vast, and the roads linking them often run for hundreds of miles with barely a bend to break the monotony. ▷

Luckily the 350 miles to Wilcannia was all straight tarmac highway, and once we got them all safely hushed down, our truck and trailer (for Nugget, Frankie and the camels) and Land-Rover (for Paddy and me) managed it with only one breakdown on the way.

To Cooper Creek

Wilcannia, some 300 miles southeast of Cooper Creek as the crow flies, is a former paddle-steamer port on the Darling River. It lies about eighty miles upstream from Menindee, where Burke, coming from Melbourne, had established his storage depot. For us, coming from Sydney, Wilcannia was a logical overnight stop on our way to the Creek.

The night was bitterly cold and the moon well up when we reached town. The hotels, not altogether surprisingly, were unable to accommodate camels, so we eschewed the comfort of warm beds in favour of the outback's starry mantle. We unloaded the camels by the light of the headlights a short distance back along the road, a process we had been dreading but which went without a hitch. We rolled out our swags around the fire, and fortified ourselves against the cold wind with meat pies and rum before turning in. The fire burned out during the night and the thermometer showed two degrees below zero at first light. Thick ice on the water troughs indicated that the temperature may have been lower still.

Loading the camels onto the truck proved just as difficult as it had been at Dubbo. After that we paused in town to make last-minute phone calls and buy a few bits and pieces. Eventually we got the show on the road, heading northwards for Tibooburra on a narrow dirt track parallel to Burke's route. Arriving in the tiny opal-mining settlement of White Cliffs at midday, we paused to ask directions. No one seemed to know for certain which was the track to Tibooburra, so we took a consensus of local opinion and headed blindly off.

Road maps in this part of the world are worse than useless; ours showed a nice straight graded road, but our two-vehicle convoy soon found itself on a rough bush track which wound across dust flats and up over endless dunes until it finally faded out into a fan of old, divergent tyre tracks.

We pressed on bravely, until at dusk we topped the red dunes which form the southern shore of the Bulloo Overflow. Once a dry mud plain, for the last few years it had been full of water, forming an inland sea which had cut off Tibooburra from the east, unless one went over the dunes. We ground our way around it in the gathering dark, picking up car tracks for a while and then losing them again.

Just as it seemed we were destined to camp in the dunes for the night, our headlights picked up a road ahead. We bumped down onto it and, tired and hungry, followed it the fifty or so dusty miles into Tibooburra.

This was one of the most pleasant little settlements in the outback: its position on the edge of beyond lent it a frontier atmosphere where everyone must help everyone else. Up near Tibooburra, if you pulled up to stretch your legs the first car to go by would stop and make sure nothing was wrong. True to form, everyone in the old Family Hotel turned out to help us unload the camels, who behaved perfectly and gave Paddy and me enough time for a cold beer before bed. Nugget, like many Aborigines, rarely took alcohol. Frankie did not drink alcohol at all. That was his personal decision—it is true that alcoholism is a serious problem in the Aboriginal population, but it is also true that many young Aboriginal men are turning back to their traditional ways and shunning alcohol.

The Seasons of Cooper Creek

▲ A rare glimpse of the waters of Cooper Creek in full spate, heading inland towards Lake Eyre. Pelicans have congregated on the far side for a spot of fishing.

AS THE TRAVELLER heads west from the base of the Great Divide in eastern Australia, all the land around, except for a few hills, appears to be flat. Only on reaching one of the great rivers of Central Australia, such as Cooper Creek (as the historical Cooper's Creek is now officially known), would the traveller realise that the ground does, in fact, gradually slope downwards. For Cooper Creek's sprawling network of channels, rather than flowing back east towards the sea, follows the slope of the land towards Lake Eyre in South Australia, the lowest point on the whole continent at nearly 40 feet below sea level.

Sometimes Lake Eyre grows huge—its two parts covering a total area of 6,600 square miles—but it regularly dwindles away to almost nothing, because of lack of water from Cooper Creek and other rivers. In most years, Cooper Creek is little more than a broad string of ponds separated by tracts of parched riverbed. But debris caught high up in the branches of surrounding trees bears testimony to occasional dramatic floods. At such times Cooper Creek can swell to fill an area that at some points reaches 50 miles wide. Desert flowers, long deprived of moisture, spring to life, and thirsty birds and animals flock to its cool, refreshing waters.

▲ The legendary Dig Tree, its venerable boughs just touching the ground, is an enduring memorial to Burke and Wills's ill-fated journey.

Even so, all of us, I think, dreamt that night of interminable dunes and mulga (acacia) scrub, rising and falling drunkenly in the beams of the headlights.

The wide main street and the row of old stone houses appeared to me in the light of dawn like an apparition from the last century, even down to the solitary donkey wandering across the street in a cloud of flies. Tibooburra had two hotels, and local tradition dictated that after a few drinks in one, you wandered over and had a few in the other; so we left the Family Hotel and followed the donkey and tradition across to the other, the Tibooburra, for breakfast.

Fortified, and with our spare petrol drums full, Paddy and I led the way north across the rolling treeless downs to the Queensland border. An hour or so beyond the border the countryside changed, and the track wound across a clay flood plain on which myall scrub—another type of acacia looking rather like miniature silver–grey weeping willows—flourished. Then the first dunes and deep channel crossings appeared. These latter consisted of soft wet sand, and we hit the first one unprepared and found ourselves bogged to the axles. The next hour or so was spent digging the Land-Rover out of the bog and cutting scrub to lay under the tyres.

We stood hot and sweaty on the far bank of the bog for another hour waiting for Nugget and Frankie, who had been following behind us and had had to pull up and refuel from the spare fuel drum a couple of times. We managed to winch them across without too much trouble and pressed on again, finally arriving at the ice-cold waters of Cooper Creek long after nightfall.

Cooper Creek is a watercourse that drains a huge part of central and western Queensland and flows into the desert country of South Australia. At most times it is a dry sandy riverbed with deep rocky waterholes here and there, but occasionally, following monsoon rains to the north, it carries vast torrents of water across country that may not have seen rain for many years. No settlement is located by the creek itself, and the nearest trading post is miles downstream. It was a weary team which lay down to rest that night, but we had decided to have a day's break here while the equipment was finally assembled, so we slept soundly.

The original Dig Tree still stands today, a gnarled old coolabah scarred with the tragic inscription, although the bark has grown over most of the letters now. It was easy to see why Burke had chosen that spot as a campsite, high on the bank of the big Bullo Bullo Waterhole, shaded by coolabahs and river red gums, and with good grazing on the flats nearby.

The banks are steep and covered in thick green lignum bush, above which countless thousands of parrots fight for perches in the tall trees. The waterhole is teeming with fish, providing a haven for the pelicans, herons and cormorants that abound on the creek.

Our one day's break for preparation here soon became two, what with the packing and repacking and the shedding of all those things which, although they might come in handy, were not absolutely essential. Even some of the food had to be abandoned, including a pile of biltong (sun-dried salted beef) and a couple of sides of bacon, dried fruit and beans. Paddy and I had heated arguments.

'Hang on to that,' I'd tell him. 'It could come in handy.'

'Handy for you, mate, but not for the poor bloody camel that's got to carry it.'

▲ Pelicans, with their enormous pouched beaks, are among Australia's most bizarre-looking birds. They use their beaks for scooping fish out of the water, and it looks as if the leaders in this hungry flock have struck lucky.

That night I lay awake stiff and sore for some time, wondering what the family was doing at home, and, more to the point, what the hell I was doing. I loved my zoo job in the city, its challenge and variety. As Curator of Mammals, one day I would be formulating chimpanzee diets, and the next I would be grappling with the problems of moving a hippopotamus. The job carried pressures, of course—my keepers thought they were overworked and my board members thought we were overstaffed—but what worthwhile job didn't carry pressures? And in any case, what on earth were all those people getting up to in my absence? In short, what had possessed me to take time off from a fine career and come all this way out here, only to find myself lying on a claypan in the icy wind of the desert night, wrapped up in an old navy overcoat?

Pulling that overcoat closer around me I shivered and thought of my warm bed at home; I dozed fitfully, telling myself that I had 1,600 miles ahead of me.

A group of tourists enjoys a leisurely trek through attractive outback country. Some treks are mini-expeditions, lasting 40 days or more.

Players race for the ball in a frantic game of camel polo—an inventive use of an animal not best known for its agility! ▶

In this 19th-century engraving, camels are seen pulling a carriage belonging to the famous coaching company Cobb and Co. Riding one of the camels is an Afghan camel handler. ▼

◀ Camels here fulfil their traditional role as long-distance pack animals on an expedition in 1906 to find a route through Western Australia.

Ships of the Australian Desert

Most non-Australians, asked to name the wild animals most typical of Australia, would probably settle for the kangaroo or the koala, but few would mention the camel. Yet Australia is home to 25,000 of them—the only wild dromedaries left in the world, in fact.

The first Australian camels were imported from India and Afghanistan in the 1840s for use in the outback. Their stamina and ability to go for long periods without water made camels suitable for all sorts of work: they carried mail and goods to isolated settlements; they transported explorers far into the interior; sometimes they were even used in place of horses to pull carriages.

With the advent of the internal combustion engine, however, camels became redundant. Many were released into the outback, where they began breeding successfully. Despite their large size—they are easily Australia's largest animals—they have done little damage to their environment: their broad, soft feet do not break up the soil to cause erosion, unlike the hard hooves of the wild horses, or brumbies, that also roam much of the interior.

Australia's relationship with the camel has now turned full circle, for the descendants of those that were originally imported are now being re-domesticated and exported to the Middle East and Africa. Camels are also used for leisure and sport: tourists can take camel treks into the outback, and camel polo, sometimes known as po-camel-lo, is increasingly popular. The length of the games is variable: as one expert put it, it 'depends on the behaviour of the camels on the day'!

▲ Wild descendants of the first camels imported to Australia 150 years ago. Camels are able to eat thorny or bitter plants in the outback that other animals won't touch. Despite their large size, camels cause little damage to the thin soil, having soft feet (*inset*) instead of hooves.

CHAPTER 2

The Land of Stone

WE LEFT THE DIG TREE CAMP on July 22, a fine cool morning. The truck drivers, who were to take our vehicles back to civilisation, and a small group of tourists in a Land-Rover gave us a rousing farewell, as did the film crew from the Australian Broadcasting Commission, who were sponsoring our trip and were there to shoot a television documentary about it. It should have been an exciting moment, but I was so worried about the food we were being forced to leave behind that frankly I felt no elation.

For once Cooper Creek was running fast and was two feet deep over the crossing. It was ice cold, and I had it on good authority that camels were reluctant to cross water. Maybe they sensed my apprehension, for they broke file as we approached the river and formed a tangle of ropes and baggage, kicking and bucking all over the place. We managed to dismount safely and sort them out after much cursing. Then we led them on foot towards the river, which they forded without a moment's hesitation, much to my relief.

We paused to fill the two drinking-water tanks, then set off. Our tanks were modern copies of 19th-century ones designed for pack camels. Each one held about twelve gallons—enough to last the four of us from four to seven days, depending on the temperature. But the copies were based on old faded photographs and the detail was not right, as we were to discover later to our cost.

The team head off into a timeless landscape that almost 120 years earlier witnessed the passage of Burke and Wills. ▶

Our route lay due west, parallel to Cooper Creek. For about half a mile on either side of the creek periodic floods had left fertile topsoil on which grew a profusion of grasses and herbs. The most visible were great expanses of verbena, whose aromatic pinkish flowers were supposedly once used in love potions. Above these towered coolabah trees, their bark amber-coloured up to about fifteen feet, then sprouting snow-white branches and beautiful dusty-blue leaves. Unfortunately this lush area soon gave way to a high stony plateau, devoid of life but for dead-looking grass and the odd bit of saltbush. Away to the south the plateau petered out into sand dunes, and to the northeast stood a range of barren peaks.

The going was slow and was interrupted by the camels continually breaking pace, causing saddle straps, baggage clips and tempers to give way. Our order of march was for either Paddy or me to walk out front, leading the other mounted on Ginger, while Nugget and Frankie rode at the back, ready to round up any camel which broke away. Paddy's and my saddles were new, as were our boots, so blisters soon started to appear on heels and bottoms.

With one of us leading and one riding, conversation between Paddy and me was almost impossible, the few words shouted to each other above the wind only serving to underline the silence. Nugget and Frankie were separated from us not only by the length of the camel train but also by barriers of language and culture. Nugget's tongue was Pitjantjatjara, from the Petermann Ranges region, but Frankie's mother had been from a neighbouring central Australian tribe that spoke Aranda. Since Frankie had lived with her for much of his life, he had few words of his father's principal language. In any case, they talked little together while in the saddle. In general, since Paddy spoke a few words of Aranda, and Nugget a few words of English, we used an outwardly incomprehensible combination of English, Pitjantjatjara and Aranda.

We made camp that night in a solitary group of stunted gums on a vast claypan, only fourteen miles from the Dig Tree. Already we had fallen into the routine we would continue for the rest of the trip. Every man was responsible for his own swag; as for the rest, Frankie would get firewood (he and his father could get a fire going in half the time it took Paddy and me), while Paddy fixed broken straps or other bits and pieces and I did the cooking, helped by Nugget who mixed and kneaded the 'damper'—a substantial slab of yeastless dough rather like Irish soda bread.

The following day we broke camp at 8.30am, and crossed our first sand dunes shortly afterwards. The camels handled the dunes well, but I became slightly anxious when I saw the poisonous crotalaria bush growing out of the sand. I need not have worried, for we later found that the camels would not touch it. The standard book on Australia's toxic plants ran to 684 pages; the fact that only about thirty of the species it listed occurred in the regions we would be traversing was of little comfort to me.

The sand dunes soon gave way to rolling gibber downs, interspersed with stony bluffs. (Gibbers—pronounced with a hard 'g'—are loose stones, produced when heat shatters the rock-hard surface layer which often forms in these

▲ Lush grass soon gave way to sand dunes and then to these unforgiving gibbers—hard, sharp stones that cover vast areas of the desert.

deserts; many have sharp edges that can cut an unwary foot.) Nevertheless that day we settled into a steady pace, and for the first time I realised what a camel team can do when they get into their rhythm: walking alongside the team I was taking three paces to their one.

A couple of times that morning I noticed a strange shifting white mass up ahead. However, it always seemed to keep miles away, vanishing and reappearing at odd intervals. Shortly after lunch, as we topped yet another stony rise, we sighted one much closer, a whirling mass of white and pink. By now we were so intrigued that we stopped and wasted a precious twenty minutes getting the binoculars unpacked. It was worth it. Through the glasses we could make out thousands and thousands of cockatoos, pink-bodied galahs and little white corellas, shifting group by group across the plain, showing their brilliant colours in flight, then almost disappearing on the ground.

The ruined hospital at Innamincka. In the last century the town was a customs post for trade between Queensland and South Australia, but after federation in 1901 customs were no longer necessary. Work at a local gas field has encouraged a handful of people to return in recent years.

Although they are quite common in the outback, what brought the corellas and galahs to that particular area we never did discover, for the ground, when we finally reached it, seemed just like the rest of the surrounding country. Perhaps the grass seeds or whatever it was had been completely cleaned up as the vast flocks moved on.

The camels, fresh and now settled into their long swinging stride, made short work of the last sixteen miles to Innamincka, and by 2.30pm we were within sight of the town. For a while last century it had been a thriving settlement with a hotel, hospital and police station, but it was later abandoned. Today it stirred again: its new pub and Mike Steele's Trading Post stood amid old stone ruins and heaps of broken bottles, but it boasted little else.

To emulate exactly the ordeal of Burke and Wills would have called for total abstinence, but a couple of beers before we faced the desert would make little difference to our total calorie intake over three months. So beer it was, and some sweets for Frankie.

The day's trek had exposed the inadequacies of our water tanks. Not only did they rub the camels' backs but one of them had already sprung a leak, needing running repairs with the last of Paddy's chewing gum. We were obliged to buy two water bags and, armed with these, we set out for a good campsite on the far side of the Mulkonbar Waterhole, only a few miles away. At this point the creek was barely four inches deep. Even so, all the curses we could muster would not get the camels across. They simply refused to go near the water, despite the fact that they'd happily walked through much deeper water two days previously.

We tried each camel in turn, and each in turn refused in its characteristic way. Alice, firmly but gently, turned away; Ginger roared, bucked and spat all over me; Larrikin nearly emasculated Paddy with a well-aimed kick. Walloper stood stock still ignoring all efforts to budge him, his eyes fixed on Mecca or some other distant object. Paddymelon bolted back towards Innamincka, while Frances and Cleo got hopelessly tangled in a lignum bush. It was a fiasco, but twenty minutes later, hot and puffing, we had them back in order.

By now the sun had almost set and the water, which had shone like a mirror before, was now in shadow. The camels crossed it like lambs.

A blazing fire and a hot bowl of biltong soup restored our spirits and, just to show that *we* weren't scared of the water, we walked back through it for a last cold beer before facing the Stony Desert. It proved to be a wise precaution.

The Stony Desert

We woke with the first light of dawn and with a terrible sense of apprehension. In the 19th century it had been customary for explorers to name each new feature after somebody important, but when the famous Australian explorer Charles Sturt came to this region north of Cooper Creek, he found it so inhospitable that he named it simply the Stony Desert. And this was *it*.

I dragged myself out of the swag with that 'Well, here goes' feeling I have experienced when running onto a football field for a grand final or when making the initial incision of a difficult veterinary operation—a mixture of excitement and dread.

Faced with this prospect, it is no wonder that the 19th-century explorer Charles Sturt named the area the Stony Desert. Posterity has credited him with its discovery and it is now called the Sturt Stony Desert. ▼

Floods like this forced the team to make their first divergence from the route of Burke and Wills, who found this same area dry when they came to it. ▶

We filled our water bags and tanks in preparation for the arid country ahead. Burke had gone west before turning north by west, thus avoiding much of the stone. We could not follow, for floods to the west had turned the Coongie Lakes into an inland sea. So, for the first time, a divergence from Burke's route was imperative. We had to head due north.

It was 9.30am before we got under way, every strap and buckle checked and nervously double-checked. For the first mile or so all was grand, the track meandering through stunted eucalypt scrub on a plain of alluvial clay. But abruptly, as we topped a low rise, we found ourselves facing the sea of stone which Sturt described as 'a stony desert covered with flints from one to six inches long which wore down the hooves of the horses almost to the quick'.

That day went badly. Ginger, in the lead, turned aside to graze each tiny piece of saltbush or succulent parakeelya he happened to pass. When this happened the other camels would pile up behind him in disarray, and Alice, thinking it was a scheduled stop, would promptly kneel, one or another of the others following suit.

About midday, just when the camels were again falling into a reasonable rhythm, there was a great crash from halfway down the line, sending all the animals into a plunging frenzy. Walloper and a water tank had parted company: a clip had given way, sending the full tank crashing onto the stone. As we dismounted to retrieve it we saw a large dark stain spreading over the red earth; our precious water was rapidly soaking away. Paddy repaired the hole as well as he could, stemming the flow to a trickle, and after tying the tank on with rawhide we were eventually under way again.

On the western horizon ran a long sand dune while to the east stood a range of low, barren hills, blue and blurred by the heat haze. In between spread the vast plain of stone. Our progress was hard and slow, Ginger stopping at every bush in sight. Walloper's load, one side lightened by a half-empty water tank, was considerably lopsided, and the full tank on the other side hung so low it had severely chafed the poor beast's knee. Rearranging the load as best we could, we only succeeded in chafing his other knee. With bitter regret, we emptied out half of the water from the sound tank to even his load, seriously reducing our capacity.

We camped that night in a washaway—a dry gully carved out of the stone by flood erosion—defended when we arrived by a small brown wren whose call closely resembled a bellbird. Sore and weary, we dined on damper, curried peas and pork and copious soggy rice—a creation rarely mentioned by gourmets but a firm favourite in the desert.

Afterwards we shared a game of 'five-hundred'—a card game in which I used to sit bemused while the three other players took my money in turn. Nugget, the poor innocent from the desert, was the worst offender. Then, wrapped in balaclava and bluey coat against the freezing night winds, I took my star sightings, updated the navigation log and marked up our exact position on the map before turning in. It was a procedure I had planned to carry out regularly—how can modern man have peace of mind if he does not know where he is?—but in fact as the trip went on this seemed less and less important. We knew we were in the desert, and travelling north; which particular part of the desert we were in soon became immaterial.

Having taken stock of the state of beasts, tanks and harness, we had decided to stay the following day and repair our gear. So at dawn we were up treating saddle sores, patching and readjusting packsaddles, and testing our equipment. We had an old and venerable Winchester rifle which was shooting true, but my revolver jammed on a faulty round, and rather than take a chance on carrying it like that we buried it in the bank of the washaway. It was a sad moment for me, as the revolver had been a gift from my father.

▲ Colourful blooms like this pink parakeelya testify to recent rainfall in the desert. The plant stores as much of the precious water as it can in small, bulbous leaves.

Frankie was the marksman of our group, with additional skills in tracking and stalking. Mostly he saw little point in our venture, in all this effort to 'chase up some fellas dead long time', but if game came in sight he was transformed instantly into an alert and formidable hunter. Paddy was a reasonable shot too, far better than I, so the two of them did the hunting.

Over a billy of tea the talk drifted from crook revolvers to crook camels and to Ginger in particular. Camels are related to cattle inasmuch as they chew the cud, and thus camel bridles cannot have a bit, because it would interfere with their chewing. The lack of a bit means that a straying or troublesome camel cannot be given the same 'gentle reminder' as a horse, and so they are often 'nose-pegged'—that is to say, one nostril is pierced and a wooden peg inserted, to which a rope or driving rein is attached.

When this practice started is uncertain, but it has been used for thousands of years in the Middle East, and the ritual procedures were taught to Nugget's father by one of the expert cameleers known in Australia as Afghans. Muslim camel handlers had originally accompanied the animals imported back in the 19th century. Although such men might well be from India or Turkey or the Yemen, they became universally known as Afghans. Being non-European, they were regarded as a necessary evil, to be discriminated against whenever possible—in some states, for example, they could neither bring their wives with them nor own land.

We decided that Ginger would have to be nose-pegged in order to stop him disrupting progress at every second saltbush. Paddy went to unpack a peg while Nugget rummaged through his swag and produced an evil-looking 'pegging stick'. I took one look at this device and offered to do the job myself, using a nice sterile scalpel, disinfectant and a local anaesthetic.

▲ Say 'cheese'! This camel is not just pulling a face, but is chewing the cud, which it would be unable to do with a conventional bit in its mouth. Instead, it has been nose-pegged to allow the rider to steer it.

Nugget declined the offer, and said that knives had been tried years ago but caused too much bleeding. I had a closer look at the pegging stick and saw his point. A scalpel was so sharp it cut whatever it crossed, blood vessels included. The wooden stick was blunt by comparison: it pierced the skin but pushed large blood vessels aside. This principle is in fact used extensively in modern surgery, and is termed 'blunt dissection'.

We decided to do it the 'proper Afghan way', but made one concession to modernity by thoroughly disinfecting the pegging stick. Paddy returned with a small wooden nose-peg, the shape of a chess bishop and over another billy (this being a rest day, we had several billies) he and Nugget explained to me the reasons for its size and shape: it had to be strong enough so that a moderate tug did not break it, yet weak enough so that if the line was caught in a tree, the peg would snap rather than have its broader base pulled through the unfortunate beast's nose. Thus the shaft had to be neither too thick nor too thin but just so. The type of wood was also important: it had to be of intermediate strength and

free of irritant resins. Metal pegs had been tested, but they got too hot in the sun and burned the nose, while plastic pegs were too hard. As the smoke drifted up I wondered how many hours around ancient campfires had been spent over this same discussion.

Eventually Ginger was roped and tied tight, and amazingly the operation was over in a moment. It was certainly no more cruel than inserting nose-rings in bulls or pigs, and less traumatic than docking horses' and dogs' tails—procedures that have little justification other than the whim of fashion. Ginger, however, was not impressed, and roared his distaste across the plain.

After a meagre lunch—a stick of biltong and a piece of damper each—Paddy decided to improve our diet by going shooting. As this seemed to the rest of us to be a complete waste of time in these parts, Nugget and Frankie curled up for a kip beside the fire, I checked out the radio, and Paddy went hunting alone. Paddy was like that—not so much an optimist as a believer in perseverance. Go at life hard enough, he reckoned, and things would turn out the way you wanted.

We settled back to rest and were dozing fitfully, plagued by flies, when wild war whoops awoke us. Paddy had triumphed: he had shot an emu. Frankie raced out to help him drag it into camp. Amid a cloud of flies old Nugget expertly sliced off the prime meat, carefully scraping the fat from the inside of the skin along the back. He heated this fat in the frying pan to release the oil, and then fried the best cuts of meat in it; the rest was boiled up in the billies. I found the meat delicious—black and a bit stringy but rich and gamy, a great improvement on biltong—but I never quite brought myself to eat the Aborigines' most prized portion, the claws.

That night, with a full stomach of fried and boiled birdie, and a billy full for tomorrow, we slept soundly.

The next day we were raring to go; not so the camels. Walloper responded to my efforts to hush him with a lightning-fast kick to my stomach, his standard response to most things. Ginger topped that by regurgitating a couple of gallons of digestive juices and half-digested herbage over Frankie and me. Spitting and regurgitation are typical defence mechanisms of the species and both the yellow–green colour and the sour smell are hard to wash off.

We hit the road late. Immediately the desert silence and stillness seemed to close in and engulf us. We could have been the only living things on this earth; nothing else stirred from horizon to horizon. To the east the mountains were closer now, jagged, jumbled piles of bare rock, glinting occasionally in the sun like suburban rooftops.

The going was hard and for the first time the pace was telling, but by now we had got Ginger to concentrate on his walking rather than on wayside snacks, and the others followed his example. We had to reach Patchawara Bore by nightfall, as that was the only water before Tooroowatchie Waterhole, fifty miles away. It was last light when the sails of the Patchawara windmill appeared ahead. We hastened toward them much relieved, only for our spirits to sink as quickly as they had risen, for the bore was dry and long abandoned, the windmill a rusted creaky skeleton.

We now faced a dilemma, as we had only a couple of days' supply of water left. I had planned to go north by northwest, following the dunes to Tooroowatchie Waterhole, a day's march away. But if that was dry too, or if by some misfortune we missed it, we would scarcely have enough water left to reach the waterhole at the Cordillo Downs cattle station.

We held a campaign conference. By going northeast, a roundabout route and longer by one day's march, we ought to strike water at a couple of supposedly good waterholes the next day. As we were still feeling our way, I decided on this safer course.

Desperate for Water

The following day we headed out at 8.30, and did twenty-seven-and-a-half miles. Creek after creek, bore after bore, dam after dam were dry. We were in dire straits.

The country was now more sandy, and scattered mulga and myall scrub started to appear again. The dry creekbeds we crossed every four or five miles

▲ Windmills are a common sight in the dry outback. They provide the power to pump precious underground water up through bores to the surface.

were lined by a curious tree with drooping blue–grey leaves and a scaly bark of brilliant red hanging in tatters like a coarse wool. Nugget or Frankie occasionally pointed out the tracks of emu and dingo, and, miles from anywhere, the tracks of a barefoot child. They were a week or more old so we didn't investigate further, but I have often wondered about them since.

Frequently on the trip Nugget made vain efforts to teach me the finer points of tracking. He would point out a track, and I would look at it and identify it as dingo. Most times I would be right but he wanted more. It was not just any dingo, it was a big old dingo heading in a certain direction late yesterday afternoon. At that time of day he would have been heading for water. The track did not just mean dingo to him, it meant water in that direction.

I remembered once long ago walking through the back streets of Athens hopelessly lost, and not being able to speak more than a couple of words of Greek. There were signposts everywhere but I could not read them, just as there were signs everywhere here in the desert if only I could decipher them. Nugget would show me how a little dust was scattered on top of the pressed print, how the wind last night had blown a little off the sharp edge of the print, how sand in front of one print was moister than the sand around it, and so on. But it was an art acquired over many years, difficult to pick up overnight, and just as difficult to teach. Paddy claimed that Nugget could 'track a dirty thought across a dry rock'. It was a pretty fair comment.

That night the dingoes howled all round us, and possibly because of this by dawn the camels had wandered out of sight and sound. (We always hung a camel bell round the neck of one of them to help us locate them in the morning.) They were loosely hobbled, so that they could look for fodder, but this also allowed them to stray some distance overnight. I felt a moment of panic, but Nugget quickly found their tracks to the south and went after them, and we were soon under way.

Within hours our first bore came in sight, but after so many disappointments we waited before getting too excited. Just as well: the first sip nearly made Paddy ill. It was salty, and salt bores such as this contained not just common salt

▲ The *Acacia cyperophylla*, one of many hundreds of species of acacia, is characterised by its red, flaky bark.

(sodium chloride) but magnesium salts also, which caused diarrhoea and increased water loss. Camels, however, could handle high levels of salinity and ours drank the briny water with relish. They could drink twenty gallons at one go, and their noisy contented slurpings did little to help relieve our thirst.

Beside the windmill was a thatched grass 'wurlie' or shelter hut, probably put together by an Aboriginal stockman. Judging by the amount of bird droppings inside, it had not been used by him for a long time.

Earlier in the day Nugget said he had seen 'dust from motor car' ahead, but as that seemed unlikely, and as neither Paddy nor I, with our younger eyes, could make out anything in the distant haze, we forgot about it. But now, sure enough, up came a four-wheel drive, bearing the emblem of the South Australian Police. As is the custom in those parts, they stopped for a yarn, enquired about our trip and gave us some idea of the terrain ahead.

They seemed quite interested in our navigation, asking us exactly where we were, how far we had come, what provisions we had, whether our radio was working and many other questions, all in a friendly, conversational sort of way. Later we discovered that the meeting was far from accidental. In fact, having heard of our trip they had set out to locate us, and, if not satisfied with our ability to survive, they had planned to dissuade us from continuing.

We must have satisfied them, however, as they gave us their last and most precious possessions—four nearly cold cans of beer, which we dispatched in an instant, Frankie alone abstaining. He would have welcomed a cold drink as much as any of us, but he had his principles. I wonder how many white lads would have held out in similar circumstances.

The younger of the two policemen had been engaged in a long, animated conversation with Nugget, whose face had creased in a gleaming, Santa Claus smile. As the four-wheel drive disappeared in a cloud of dust and good wishes on both sides, Nugget told me that the policeman was a 'proper number one fella': he had addressed him by his correct title—'*chilbi*', or elder—and had spoken to him in his own language! He was obviously deeply touched by this rare courtesy in a white man, so much so that his 'white man's name' was now dropped, and he was Chilbi to all of us from there on.

This is not some exotic hat but a thatched roof made from grasses, which a Pitjantjatjara woman is carrying over to place on a 'wurlie', a type of shelter also made from woven grass. ▼

We were to find that the police in these remote regions tended to be like these two: good bushmen with a real interest in the area and in the well-being of its isolated inhabitants. Their range of duties was impressive, from postman to fire chief, mechanic to insurance assessor, stock inspector to radio repairer and back to policeman again on Saturday nights. We were sorry to say goodbye to them.

The country ahead was beautiful, consisting of high red sandhills dotted with green and blue bushes and scattered with yellow and white wild flowers. The dunes were interspersed with clay flats covered in Mitchell grass and the occasional dried-up swamp marked by curiously twisted apple-gums. Here in these flats the bird life was abundant: finches, silver-eyes and flocks of budgerigars were everywhere.

Mitchell grass is dense, tussocky stuff, no good for fattening stock but drought resistant and useful as roughage for the survival of cattle during severe dry periods. In general the open plains of Australia look as if they could offer man absolutely nothing to help him survive. But around the campfire Chilbi would show us some twig or leaf or head of grass he had spotted that day and explain how his people used it, the season it could be eaten, the parts to eat and the method of preparation, and how it could be distinguished from other similar but poisonous vegetation. Like many of my academic colleagues, I had always thought of the hunter-gatherer's life as relatively simple. How wrong I was.

▲ A shimmering cloud of budgerigars takes advantage of a rare expanse of water. Most people outside Australia only know budgies as solitary caged birds, but huge flocks like this are a common sight in their native country.

The countryside was pretty here and the going soft, but we had to keep going all the way to the next bore, Bloodwood Well, for now we were almost completely out of water, our ration that day having been just four mouthfuls per man.

The sergeant, the elder of the two police, had warned us that Bloodwood was very hard to find, being in a tiny valley completely surrounded by high dunes. He was right. It turned out to be impossible to spot unless you knew exactly where it was. To be on the wrong side of the right dune and miss the well by fifty yards was as good as being ten miles off. But we need not have worried: by watching the game trails Chilbi took us straight to it, just on dusk. Unfortunately, one look at the salty crust around the tank told us all we needed to know. We had no alternative now but to press on to Cordillo Downs and hope our meagre remaining water supply got us there.

The Seventh Day

As I walked I settled back into my now constant daydream, a big cascade in the midst of lush jungle, with a deep waterhole beneath it, crystal clear and icy cold. Occasionally there was a beautiful woman in the pool, but more often there was just me with my enamel mug.

My reverie was shattered by the startled voices of Chilbi and Frankie behind me. They were pointing excitedly to the east. I looked in that direction and saw a pair of brolgas taking off, elegant grey cranes about five feet high, seldom seen so far south. Even more interesting, when we got there, was the tiny muddy soak the birds had taken off from, lying at the base of a gigantic dune.

Trying to filter out as much mud as was humanly possible, we boiled both billies for hours, and as we drank cup after cup of tea, we filled the water bags for tomorrow. The journal we kept describes our fare that night as 'mud curry'. Indeed, curry powder turned out to be one of the best things we had packed. It was light and it could cover up the taste of mud—not to mention biltong, which got very boring, or even pork when it was slightly rotten.

We hoped the brolgas would return, but they never did. These birds are nature's ballerinas and their stage is the plains. They dance in pairs or groups, never alone, leaping high in the air with wings outstretched to catch the breeze so that they can float gently back to earth, their slender legs meanwhile

With consummate grace, a brolga bows to a potential mate. Such 'dancing', however, is not restricted to courtship: it seems brolgas may also dance to strengthen their family bonds. ▼

describing graceful arcs beneath them. In summer the heat haze on the plains distorts and magnifies their dance to give it a mysterious, magical quality. (The most wonderful of all the Aboriginal dances I have seen is the 'Dance of the Brolgas', performed by a group from Arnhem Land in the Northern Territory.)

By now our camp was in dark shadow, but the last rays of the setting sun were lighting up the crimson dune above us. Chilbi trudged up to the top and disappeared, to return in complete darkness carrying an armful of a weedy plant I had seen growing on a dune further back. I later found out that this bush is the pitchery plant which, when dried, is smoked or chewed by the Aborigines as a mild intoxicant. For the next few days the loads of a couple of the camels were decorated with the leaves Chilbi had collected, drying in the sun. Pitchery induces a state of inner tranquillity and can be used to overcome fatigue and thirst on a long trek—as well as the pain of initiation ceremonies such as circumcision. Chilbi told us it was sometimes used to 'lace' a small waterhole so that the animals that drank there became stupefied and would stand quietly while Aboriginal hunters approached and despatched them.

That night the dunes around the camp protected us from the dreadful winds that howled ceaselessly across the stony plain and had almost frozen us at our last few camps. Even so, the thermometer went as low as 2°C at midnight. This wind seemed to cut through blankets and swags to numb our very marrow, and by day it dried and cracked our lips and sunburnt faces.

The next morning we were away at dawn, and, after a few more miles of narrow clay flats weaving below the high dunes, the country gave way to a plain of hard, sharp stones the size of a man's fist. Even in our thick-soled boots it was hellish going, so we were prepared to be pretty understanding about the camels' slower pace.

We had been going a week now from the Dig Tree, and it was time to take stock. That kept my mind busy as we carefully stepped our way between the gibbers. The stores were not working out too well. We had counted on living off the land quite a bit, but there seemed to be little game about; according to the old records of the early pastoral companies and the pioneers before them, there never had been an abundance of kangaroo or emu in these parts. We were eating our dried meat at a high rate, and had left much of it behind anyway. Sugar, which I had planned to use at the rate of one teaspoon per cup of tea, went at half a handful per cup, and many cups we had—sweet billy tea was a great brew for the thirsty and weary. Also, water problems had forced us further east than we had planned, adding to the total distance.

All in all, though, things were not working out too badly. On the plus side, the camels were behaving well on stone that was worse than anything we had expected. In the first week we had covered 116 miles, much of which had been across stone like this. The equipment was working too, and our team was falling into a good daily routine. Chilbi and Paddy would get up before dawn and set off to bring in the camels, while Frankie and I (the sleepyheads) would boil the billy, roll up the swags and pack away the cooking gear, setting aside the lunch pack and filling up the water bags from the tanks for the day. (This was vital:

A cheerful camel herdsman, his mount hushed down for unloading. The camels in the background are wild. Such camels may be captured for export or for tourist and leisure uses. ▶

water in the big metal tanks got very hot, and by midday was undrinkable, but in the canvas water bags the evaporation kept it cool.) Each made his own breakfast, a handful of rolled oats with milk powder and sugar, with a touch of water from the billy. Then all joined in the task of removing the hobbles and hushing down and saddling the camels, loading them up and tying them in line for the day's journey.

Paddy and I took turns at the dawn walk—an hour-and-a-half stretch aimed at putting as much dirt behind us as possible before the heat of the day—while the other climbed aboard Ginger and navigated. The rear was brought up by Chilbi on Alice and Frankie on Paddymelon. After the first walk we paused briefly, took off our heavy coats, gloves and balaclavas, and changed over for an hour and a half, by which time the temperature had usually warmed up to some 70°F. We would then make hourly changes till lunch. Camels do not take kindly to stopping or starting—particularly starting—so that a two-minute comfort stop could easily end up costing a quarter of an hour.

Lunch consisted of a piece of damper, some dried fruit, a cup of effervescent vitamin mix and a good lie-down for half an hour. Then on the track again until around five o'clock, when we would start scanning ahead for a suitable campsite. We looked for a site that offered good browsing for the camels, handy firewood, a flat stone-free clearing, and, if at all possible, a waterhole. Once we reached camp the camels were unloaded and hobbled as quickly as possible, while Frankie got the fire going, Chilbi made the damper, I cooked the main meal of the day—a curry or stew—and Paddy wrote up his day's notes.

Occasionally I would do a star sighting, but once camp was made and the swag unrolled, any activity was an effort, and any effort not immediately and vitally necessary was dismissed. Mostly we lay on our swags in silence, teacup in one hand, cigarette in the other, boots off and eyes staring into the warm coals and the drifting wisps of smoke.

Cordillo

Our going that morning was some of the worst we had encountered, all sharp small gibbers now that the giant red dunes lay behind us. Larrikin handled the stone badly and dragged back. Halfway through the pre-lunch stretch, though, a line of trees—coolabah and river red gum—emerged from the haze, well-watered specimens standing thirty feet or more, and beyond them gentle dunes.

On reaching the trees we saw the clear water of the Mariana Waterhole. Ducks took off at our approach, and the shoreline of the waterhole was covered with the tracks of cattle, kangaroo, lizards and small birds of all types and sizes. Our lunch was splendid that day—mostly water, and lots of it. I remember sitting on the bank and wondering who Mariana had been, and what lonely soul had thought of her as he gazed into these blue waters. It struck me that a woman is much better immortalised by a beautiful life-giving waterhole like this than by having a busy city street named after her.

After lunch we headed through some of the largest and most beautiful dunes I have ever seen. The country in between was of flat clay, and walking on it was like walking on a newly rolled tennis court. Alas, after a few hours the dunes receded to the south, and once again we found ourselves enduring the stone.

On the third hour-long walk after lunch Chilbi suddenly pointed ahead and yelled 'Station up there!' Straining our eyes we could just about make out what appeared to be a radio mast in the dancing heat haze. It had to be Cordillo! We reckoned it was no more than a couple of miles away, and our pace quickened.

They were a long couple of miles. The plain rolled on endlessly and even after the homestead itself came into sight we walked for hours.

Cordillo Downs, or Cordillo as it was called locally, was settled in the 19th century. The stone buildings at the homestead were said to have been built by Spanish stonemasons, which probably accounted for its Hispanic name. A lonelier site for a homestead could not exist— just a rocky knoll rising out of the gibber

As a full moon hovers over the plain, two of the team's camels enjoy their favourite part of the day—their regular evening browse. ▼

plains, with only the red dunes far to the south to show that the earth was not one vast sea of stone. Miraculously, below the rocky knoll lay two huge water-holes, and to these we headed.

The station manager came down and asked us to keep our camels clear of the homestead, since he was afraid his horses would bolt as soon as they smelled them. We were to be told this on many occasions, but in fact we found that, by and large, horses were not in the slightest bit worried by camels; in fact they generally raced up and had a good look before trotting off.

Shortly before we made camp a vehicle appeared and disgorged two men, Joe Judge and Joe Scherschel, photographers from the *National Geographic*, which had contributed to our trip. Having covered wars and natural catastrophes for many years, they were both veterans of the worst terrains and situations the planet had to offer, and now they were researching the history and geography of the whole outback region explored by Burke and Wills. They were here to photograph us as well, and would cross our tracks again on a few occasions. Since they were both called Joe we nicknamed them Joe-Joe as a single unit.

The extra company instilled a party spirit into our weary team. So after we had made camp on the bank of one of the big waterholes we splurged out on a big pork and sultana curry, washed down (somewhat inappropriately) with several bottles of 1972 Tyrrell's Cabernet-Sauvignon, courtesy of Joe-Joe. They were good company, and the talk flowed round the campfire that night long after the moon was up. We finally crawled, tired and contented, into our swags, having decided that tomorrow would be a rest day and that therefore, mercifully, we could sleep in. We tried to average one day off in seven, but dry wells, sick camels, tired feet and the odd visitation sometimes tempted us to vary this.

As luck would have it, though, the camels wandered down to the waterhole for a drink at dawn, and woke the thousands of noisy corellas which perch in the

Vintage Australia: A New World of Wine

WINE-MAKING is a historical tradition in European countries such as France, where grapes have been cultivated since Roman times. Yet Australia has been producing wine for over 150 years and has acquired a reputation for wines that rival some of the best Europe can offer.

As with so many of Australia's great industries, wine-making had the humblest of beginnings. A handful of European settlers first planted vines on the Liverpool Plains, now a suburb of Sydney. Those original plants are long gone, but the Sydney area still boasts one of Australia's major wine-producing regions, the Hunter Valley, where production began in 1832 with the planting of 20,000 cuttings imported from Europe.

Elsewhere, religious persecution was the unlikely precursor to the establishment of a wine industry. In the 1840s Lutherans from Germany emigrated to Australia to escape persecution for their beliefs, and were invited to settle in Barossa Valley, South Australia. These Lutherans, who were expert wine-makers, planted the first vines in 1847. Nowadays the valley is Australia's premier wine-producing region and South Australia accounts for about two thirds of the country's total output—nearly 60 million gallons from just one state!

In fertile Barossa Valley, South Australia, grape pickers carry on a local tradition begun by German Lutherans in the 1840s. ▶

trees along its banks. Thus we were up early after all, bleary-eyed and somewhat hung over, with the billy boiling, well before Orion had faded in the dawn sky. The day passed pleasantly on the thousand-and-one camp chores that wait patiently until rest days.

The owners of Cordillo, Lee and John Perry, came out and made us welcome with meat and sugar and advice on the country to the northwest. We nose-pegged Larrikin amid his deafening protests, rested before consuming grilled steak followed by boiled rice with sugar, and were later joined by Joe-Joe and some stockmen from the station. A beer cooled in the creek and lively company at the end of the rest day put us in remarkable spirits and we swagged down warmly, but only after a vital radio call.

Although rarely used and occupying precious space, our portable radio was a treasured possession—our insurance policy, for it meant that in the event of a disaster we could get in touch with flying-doctor bases anywhere from Broken Hill to the Gulf of Carpentaria. Not to have taken it would have been irresponsible, for it cost the people of the outback a lot of time and money looking for idiots who ventured unprepared into these parts telling no one where they were going, sometimes paying the ultimate penalty and dying of thirst before they were found.

That day we radioed our position to the tiny mission hospital at Birdsville, our next major port of call, and back came a reassuring reply: 'Receiving you loud and clear. Understand we will see you in seven days. Good luck, over and out.'

▲ **The Royal Flying Doctor Service of Australia provides rapid medical assistance to isolated areas. The service was first established in 1928, and to this day is a vital lifeline to those working in or just passing through the outback.**

▲ Aboriginal women, accompanied by a small child, chat while winnowing and cleaning acacia seeds. These are then ground into flour and mixed with water for baking.

This colourful spread of appetising fruits laid out on palm leaves would be typical fare for Aborigines living in Australia's tropical rain forest regions. ▶

Boomerangs—essential weapons in the Aboriginal hunter's armoury—can be straight or curved. This hunter has chosen curved (returning) ones to drive animals into an ambush. ▼

Easily overlooked by a non-Aborigine, to those who can recognise them these tracks in the sand offer vital clues to the whereabouts of the next meal—in this case a fair-sized lizard. ▼

Survival in the Wild

AUSTRALIA is one of the few remaining places on earth where one can find true isolation. Towns are often hundreds of miles apart, with nothing in between but endless parched desert. Those who visit this land ill-equipped may well never leave it, but those who actually live there, the Aborigines, learn traditional skills which complement their modern way of life.

Tracking is a skill in which the Aborigines have legendary ability. An experienced hunter can identify not only what animal made the track but how fast it was travelling and even how recently: the amount of sand blown over the track, for example, indicates whether it is hours or days old. Having tracked down an animal, the hunter has at his disposal a range of weapons for killing it. A powerful throw from a straight (non-returning) boomerang can kill instantly, but a curved (returning) boomerang can direct game into an ambush. Spears are effective both for killing game and also, in the north, for catching fish, demanding rapid reactions from the hunter or fisherman.

Game can be hard to come by in the outback, and Aboriginal women, who hunt very little, find up to 80% of their community's food by gathering such food as berries, leaves and tubers, and by catching small lizards. An additional source of protein comes from witchetty grubs, which, when baked, produce a flavour reminiscent of almonds.

▲ Spear fishing on Elcho Island, Northern Territory. A throwing stick held under the back of the spear helps extend its range.

◀ Men do most of the hunting, but women actually provide more food. Here, a woman digs to look for witchetty grubs, caterpillars which feed on tree roots.

▲ Though not exactly gourmet delicacies to European eyes, witchetty grubs are a firm favourite in the Australian desert!

CHAPTER 3

North to Birdsville

T HE MOMENT THE CORDILLO HOMESTEAD disappeared below the horizon a feeling of solitude set in and the happy company of the last night's camp became just a distant dream. Each of us trod silent across the plain, surrounded by stone and his own thoughts. Mine turned to Sturt's name for the area, Stony Desert. There was stone all through this country, but it was interspersed with sand dunes, claypans, swamps, well-grassed downs and clearly, in good seasons, lakes and rivers too. It was only in occasional isolated areas such as this that one came upon an unbroken horizon of stone.

Our trek that day revealed the scarcity of wildlife in the Stony Desert. We saw two dingoes and six hawks in the entire day's march; thus Providence Waterhole, when we reached it, was greatly appreciated, home as it was to two elegant brolgas, surrounded by flocks of budgerigars and quarrions. Quarrions, or cockatiels, are small, grey cockatoos with orange cheeks and yellow crests, very noisy and always in a hurry.

In the wild, budgerigars once occurred in flocks of hundreds of thousands across the plains of Mitchell grass, but the introduction of sheep and cattle greatly reduced the amount of seeds available, and the enormous flocks that once blacked out the sky have now dwindled to a few hundred or so. At first glance they appear to be promiscuous little creatures as they spend half their life courting, but in fact they are very faithful, and appear to mate for life.

There was a vehicle track of sorts going through from Providence Waterhole to Cadelga, but it followed the high stone country to avoid the clay and sand which become impassable in the wet. We had no need for more stone, so we headed north, leaving the road far to the east.

Only a few miles on we wondered if we had made a wise decision, as we were faced with a depressing series of rocky rises and sharply eroded gullies. The camels took to this terrain with little grace, and both Paddy and I were just about done with coercing the poor beasts as they crawled up and slipped down the steep slopes. Before our trip we had both thought of ourselves as pretty fit—I had been jogging five miles a day around the steep sandy hills of Sydney Harbour National Park and Paddy had been clearing land, felling trees and putting up fences—but none of our training had prepared us for this, and we were in fairly low spirits.

Suddenly the ridges gave way to a different scene altogether: a fabulous valley, bounded to the west by high sand dunes and to the east by a low range of hills.

▲ For many years ornithologists puzzled over whether the pretty quarrion, or cockatiel, was a type of cockatoo or a parrot, as its behaviour is typical of both groups.

Below us the valley floor was broad and flat, a claypan hidden beneath a carpet of wild flowers. In the centre a swamp was teeming with life. We hurried on.

In the distance moved herds of emu unconcerned by our intrusion, and overhead flight after flight of waterfowl accompanied us. This is the way it often is at a waterhole, even in the remotest parts of the desert. When riverbeds or claypans fill with flood water, aquatic plants soon emerge and the desiccated eggs of brine shrimps hatch in their millions, attracting birds from far and wide. The good times seldom last, though, and occasionally birds are stranded and die of thirst on the return journey, giving rise to the many stories of stockmen encountering dead swans or pelicans in the desert.

Ahead of us, ten emus ceased their foraging to watch our approach, then in their own inquisitive way, waddled straight up to us. This incredible lack of fear was evident in all the animals of that valley, and was a sign that man had not been here for a long, long time. But we were too hungry for meat to be prey to guilt complexes.

Paddy tipped his hat and grinned. 'It might as well have walked straight into our tucker bag,' he said, unpacking the rifle.

At almost point-blank range, one emu went down. The others scuttled off a few paces, but their curiosity got the better of them, and they came back one by one until we all stood in a close group, man and emu, watching Chilbi skin one of their relations. The emus minded this far less than I did. They then wandered away to inspect our camels, who were taking the opportunity to rest, and withstood their close examination with studied indifference.

If I ever return to that valley I will leave my gun behind. It almost seemed like a breach of confidence to use it. The emus padded along beside us when we got under way again, keeping us company until something else caught their interest and they pottered off. Their bizarre behaviour was quite in keeping with

◄ A carpet of blood-red wild hops stains the broad valley floor, enhancing the mauve tinge of the hills beyond.

their looks: with those quizzical eyes, and their heads moving backwards and forwards slightly out of sync with their legs as if a cog were missing somewhere, they looked completely imbecilic too.

Shortly after the emus departed Frankie yelled and pointed to a green-leaved creeper growing over the clay. Within minutes we were picking handfuls of a green grape-like fruit off the vines. I found the berries—the flesh of which tasted like passionfruit—delightful, and made a splendid lunch of them. It was nearly three hours later when the pains first started. When I realised I was in dire straits I did my first aerial dismount, heading for the cover of a small lignum bush a hundred yards away. The other three were for some reason unaffected, an injustice that bothered me as I squatted wretchedly.

Those berries could be used medicinally; they are certainly the most effective purgative I have ever known.

The Explorers and the Exploited

The valley was now widening out into a dry endless plain with tree lines marking the locations of dry creekbeds on the horizon. The heat haze lifted these stunted trees until they appeared to float above the surface like the sails of an old square-rigger. I was reminded of a trip I once made in Africa to study wildlife diseases: there, zebra and giraffe in the distance appeared to be walking about twenty feet above a shimmering silver sea.

◄ An extraordinary sea of sand, its waves—dunes patterned by the wind—harbouring in their lee narrow pockets of life.

I wondered, as I swayed gently from side to side on the camel, how the first explorers had felt. What were they looking for? What drives any explorer? An eminent Australian historian once remarked:

'Australia's explorers…were a very mixed assortment…The chief thing they had in common was devotion to adventuring…But a more potent influence was the pursuit of glory. Undoubtedly some of the land explorers had their sights firmly set on fame; and this, one may suggest, was not to their discredit, or at least only mildly so, for in practically every instance it merged with a third and deeper motive…the thrill of discovery.'

These were certainly the motives of many explorers, but whereas their daily notes are often crammed with notes of new plants, animals and mountain ranges, descriptions of new tribes or cultures, Burke kept no such diary. He raced with his camels for the Gulf of Carpentaria, determined to beat the men of Stuart's South Australian expedition, who were mounted on fast horses. In a letter to his sister Burke had written: 'I am confident of success, but know that failure is possible; and I know that failure would, to me, be ruin!' He sought glory, pure and simple, and the worst that could befall such a man was to see someone else get the glory.

It must have been a terrible let-down to be a glory-seeker in Central Australia. In Africa, explorers found lush forests, gigantic lakes, new grazing lands, strange tribes or a fortune in ivory. Père David, in Asia, traced the fabled panda to the Tibetan Himalayas. In the Americas rich prairies, gold, timber and entire new civilisations greeted the explorer. But in Australia, the further they ventured, the drier the land became, each ridge more barren than the last. There was no city of gold over the next sand dune, just more sand dunes, and the only reward was the satisfaction of being the first to reach them. Those who survived to return again and again were either dedicated explorers or simply men to whom a city office was greater torture than thirst or privation. By contrast, I suspect that Burke was neither: had he survived, it is unlikely that the outback would have seen him again.

Yet barren though it was, this landscape offered something else, something hard to define. Struggling across it like an ant across a gigantic saucer, utterly alone, under the blue dome of the sky, man was struck by the immensity of this land and made aware of his own insignificance. It would be there unchanged centuries after he was forgotten. He had discovered no glory, but something of eternity.

It is strange how mind and body and consciousness dissociate themselves from each other under these conditions, for I recall contemplating the mysteries of eternity while I stumbled over gibber, smelling of sweat and camel, and at the same time singing a dirty ditty about a legendary lass of ill repute.

Sundown brought us to a line of tall trees running from east to west along the banks of an enormous waterhole sixty-odd yards wide and miles long. The trees were alive with ibises, corellas and galahs. Unfortunately, as we made camp beneath a spreading coolabah, we were attacked by swarms of mosquitoes that did

Skeletal branches alive with roosting ibises stand in striking silhouette against the most ravishing of sunsets. ▼

not let up all night, though we kept them at bay by continually stoking the camp-fire. Even so, Paddy claimed in the morning that he had lost at least a couple of pints of blood.

The night was one of the coldest yet, the thermometer registering 2°C at dawn. We were eleven days and 190 miles out from Cooper Creek; following our detours in search of water we were now level with, though far to the east of, Burke's Camp 75. Exact precision on the journey was also hampered by the fact that Wills's journal usually mentioned latitude only and failed to mention longitude.

Since we still had the fire going, we breakfasted on fried emu and set out well fed and confident. It was probably this feeling of well-being that made me a little lax in my navigation, for we were soon lost. Our map had shown a sizable creek northeast of the waterhole, but we failed to realise that a dry gully we crossed was the creek in question, and kept heading northeast towards a line of trees which, as it turned out, marked a large dry swamp. Turning north we trudged through mile after mile of dry swamp and stony hollows (known as gilgais)—rough going indeed.

Paddy was unimpressed. 'Way we're going, mate, I reckon you'd lose yourself walking back from the bloody dunny.'

The swamp stopped abruptly at the foot of a low range, which soon gave way to sand dunes. A cooling breeze sprang up and gently stirred the numerous wild flowers. It had almost been worth getting lost to see them. On one of the dunes we picked up vehicle tracks and followed them to Cadelga. An old outstation, built around the 1880s from solid stone to withstand sieges by the Aborigines, it now stood in ruins, abandoned by man but host to a number of sleepy lizards which came out from cracks in the stonework to sun themselves.

▲ Cadelga outstation is now in ruins, revealing the fabric of its solidly built walls. These recall a time when Europeans sought to defend their settlements from attack by Aborigines angry at having their land stolen.

Historians have described Australia's frontier conflicts as the 'hidden war'. It was primarily a series of skirmishes which moved outwards as European colonisation progressed. Pitched battles were one-sided affairs due to the superiority of rifles over spears and the mobility of men on horseback. Official policy was to avoid bloodshed, so in official reports blood was never shed. There were no massacres; Aborigines were simply 'dispersed', and if they retaliated they were described as 'cowardly and treacherous'.

As a result of such official niceties, and the tactful silence of school textbooks, awkward questions hang over Australian history. In 1788 there were estimated to be 300,000 Aborigines, but by the early 20th century only 60,000 were left. (Currently there are just over 260,000.) So what happened to the others? Admittedly European diseases swept many away, and others died when livestock destroyed their food plants and waterholes or when they were moved onto the lands of other tribes who did not want them. But there is no doubt at all that, in the ruthless quest for control of land, the gun took a mighty toll too.

Over the Border

We had intended to cut west from Cadelga, as we were now well clear of the floods that had not been around in Burke's time. But bad stone lay to the west, and a chance encounter with an old-timer repairing a fence near the Cadelga ruins persuaded us to head north into Queensland. He failed to mention the bad stone that lay to the north too, so off we headed. Fools!

The team set their camp in the pink light of evening. In the background, Paddy and Chilbi tend to the camels, while Frankie keeps warm by the fire. ▶

The rest of that day, however, was good going: sand hills, claypans and masses of wild flowers, with bees and finches flitting between them. In mid-afternoon we crossed level ground covered with cane grass, so tall it almost obscured the camels. As fodder this cane was useless, but my great-grandfather thatched his mud-brick house on his first parcel of land with cane grass, swearing it made the best roof a man could have. Displaying little hesitation in pushing through it, the camels sampled as they went. Shortly after that a high fence loomed up: this was the dingo fence marking the Queensland border. We camped that night on the side of a large dune, and feasted on the remainder of the emu. Sunset was a brilliant purple, and turned the red sand dune an extraordinary colour.

As we sat round the campfire that night Chilbi produced his pitchery, collected back near Bloodwood and now dried. Out of curiosity I tried some, rolled into a cigarette with tobacco. The result was a foul taste, cough, headache and insomnia. I don't think the authorities need worry about pitchery catching on with the youth of today.

Our next day's route lay north. Across it on the map lay Shallow Lake. Most lakes in these parts are shallow at the best of times, when they aren't bone dry.

Thus I had confidently drawn our course straight across the Shallow Lake. But there really was a lake—deep, blue water miles wide surrounded by lush flats and scattered box and eucalyptus, with flocks of waterfowl resting on the banks.

As we laboriously skirted the lake to the east we were in for another, even less pleasant surprise: steep stony escarpments, not mentioned on the map. We found some maps very reliable, others hopelessly misleading. Many wells, roads and stations had been abandoned, fences pulled down and waterholes silted up; but how any map-maker could have missed gigantic stone escarpments which had been in the same spot for eternity was beyond our comprehension.

To the north of Shallow Lake (re-christened 'Bloody Deep Lake' by Paddy), we followed a large sand dune until about midday, when we crossed the track from Birdsville to the small outback community of Windorah and once again found ourselves on gibber plains. The wind, which had cooled us earlier in the dunes, now ceased, and the heat started to affect men and camels. Finally we saw up ahead the wide green plain of the Diamantina River dancing above the heat haze.

Here, a herd of magnificent wild horses, or brumbies, was going down to water at the river. These desert animals were incredibly hardy, carrying, among others, thoroughbred and Arab bloodlines. These and similar horses from other harsh regions (notably the Kimberleys in Western Australia) provided the mounts for the famous Australian Light Horse cavalry unit. It was an amazing

Brumbies: Born to be Free

BRUMBIES—Australia's wild horses—have, in their short history, become the stuff of legend and folklore. Their beauty and speed are recalled around campfires, in poems and in novels. Brumbies seem to embody the essential sense of freedom that the vast Australian outback inspires.

Brumbies are descended from various breeds of horses that came to Australia—a land with no horses of its own—with European settlers from the late 18th century onwards. During the 19th century many escaped captivity and began breeding in the wild, some on the plains and others in hill country, where they gradually became stockier in build. How these wild horses came to be called brumbies is less clear: some say they were named after one James Brumby, who allegedly released a number of horses in 1804; others believe the name derives from an Aboriginal word for 'wild'—booramby.

▲ Proud and free, brumbies symbolise the call of the wild. They are renowned for their stamina, and many will be broken in as riding horses after an annual round-up.

Around 200,000 brumbies now roam the continent, and they have had a disastrous impact on the environment. Their hard hooves break up the thin soil, causing erosion and destroying plants on which other species depend. What is more, brumbies encroach on the scant grazing for sheep and cattle. Enraged farmers used to fence off waterholes so that the trespassers died of thirst, but nowadays shooting is the preferred—and more humane—method of control.

sight to watch them whirling in a cloud of red dust across stone that would have made the average horse lame inside an hour.

Larrikin was giving so much trouble that day, pulling back or breaking file, that I would gladly have swapped him for a horse. He even managed to break his nose-peg with one of his sudden dashes. A year or so earlier he had broken his jaw, and although the bone had mended, it had left the lower jaw slightly out of line with the upper, so that it was difficult for him to chew. In the country we were going through there was precious little to eat anyway, which made his plight even worse. His condition was the cause of some concern as he was losing weight rapidly.

Off to the right we made out the roof of a building nestled at the foot of a large hill. It was a shed with a rainwater tank. The water was sweet and cool and we greedily drank our fill. It seemed strange that a drink of cold water, a bit of shade and a quiet smoke could give such pleasure, but it was strange only until you had been without for some time. We knew exactly how Burke and Wills felt when they wrote:

'Thursday, 20th December: We did not leave this camp until half past eight, having delayed to refill the water bags with the milky water, which all of us found to be a great treat again.'

The shed belonged to a homestead called Durrie, which was visible in the distance but too far out of our way, so we set out west again. As we did so a car appeared in a cloud of dust, carrying the homestead children to see the camels and an invitation to eat at the homestead that night. News of our approach had reached them over the radio. For some reason that I never discovered, Chilbi would not come; perhaps he was just plain tired. Frankie, of course, would not go without him—he was still uneasy on his own in the presence of non-Aborigines.

We camped about eight miles west of the homestead that night and our host, Jim Evans, arrived to drive us back for dinner, bringing with him a couple of large steaks each for Chilbi and Frankie. It was a memorable night, with a shower followed by two helpings each of roast beef with gravy, potato, carrots, peas, then lemon sago and custard! Colleen, our hostess, was used to feeding men who had been droving in these parts, and calmly and seriously enquired if we had had enough!

Over cups of tea the talk turned to cattle, horses, the droughts, the floods and the wildlife. It turned out our host was not only a good bushman but a dedicated naturalist who had collected many valuable specimens for museums and research institutions.

Snakes

Back at camp that night we slept like logs, dreaming of lemon sago. The camels must have been thinking of food also, for dawn found them miles away amongst the lignum bushes on the Diamantina flats, and we did not break camp until a quarter to nine. Shortly afterwards one of the Aboriginal workers from the station drove up with a present of cigarettes for Chilbi (which he didn't smoke, but we did!) and a bullock hide, invaluable for running repairs to our hard-used leather tackle. This was so large it was carried across the lap of the lead rider, either Paddy or myself. It made an excellent drum and I am sure that such was the origin of drums: simply an entire rolled hide awaiting use for clothing or whatever.

As the sun rose higher the drumming died down, for the day was fiercely hot, and the stone as bad as any we had yet crossed. Our camels had enabled us earlier to travel in a straight line over large areas of soft sand, but now we met up with the winding course of the track to Windorah again—a mass of gibbers exactly the same as all the surroundings but marked by a white stone or stake at intervals. We trudged on, and the miles went past slowly. Nothing moved around us—a state we had come to regard as normal, so that after a while my eyes kept looking at my feet just to watch movement. It was in such a mood, feet shuffling and camel chains clinking in unison, that we encountered a so-called fierce snake. This was undoubtedly Australia's most venomous snake. What with its somewhat aggressive nature (hence the name), and the fact that the venom was many times more potent than that of a tiger snake or taipan, it was not a creature to be fooled with.

▲ **Australia has more venomous snakes than any other country in the world. This one, the desert banded snake, is one of the most eyecatching.**

Thus, when Paddy noticed a long glistening shape just a few yards ahead of me, we halted to examine (and avoid) it. It was about five to six feet long, with a black head and slender bronze body, and it moved out of our way with an unhurried grace, thankfully showing none of the behaviour which its name suggested. From then on, however, I made a special effort to fix my eyes on the ground a reasonable way ahead of my own feet! We were to encounter other snakes on the journey, and many of these desert species are venomous. The desert death adder, the whip snake and the mulga are all potentially lethal. Others may not be lethal, but their venom can cause excruciating agony. On one occasion such a snake glided between Paddy and the lead camel, but neither took the slightest notice. Camels can be very phlegmatic.

The heat in that country not only came down from above, it was also reflected up from the stone below. We started to find the going heavy, and when we saw another line of stunted trees ahead in a rocky gully we decided to lunch there. Reaching it, we found a delightful little rock hole about six inches deep. The water in it seemed almost too cold to drink. All agreed to pause there for a siesta, but the flies, ants and mosquitoes made sleep impossible. Instead I sat with my feet in the water, wriggling my toes and watching the water boatmen scuttle about. After this pleasant interlude it took a major effort to get ourselves going again. It was so traumatic that we decided we simply could not afford to take siestas in future.

I cannot recall anything that afternoon except stone and heat and flopping exhausted somewhere on the plain that night, too tired even to take my boots off. We had covered thirty miles, which was all that mattered. We were fourteen days and 278 miles out from Cooper Creek—level with Burke's Camp 78 on the Diamantina River, two days' march to the west.

Next morning, I decided to help Chilbi find the camels. In the grey of dawn we set out, and searched for half an hour before we came upon them. Larrikin was in his most murderous mood that morning, lashing out, biting and doing his damnedest to break away. When we finally got them all back to camp Frankie tried to keep the rest of the camels calm, and Chilbi and I did our best to hold Larrikin while Paddy fought to hush him down and get his saddle on. Larrikin would go down, roaring and complaining, but when Paddy reached underneath him to pull the girth strap across, he would rear up again and lash out at him or at one of us. At one stage he caught me a sharp smack on the hipbone. In his usual determined fashion, Paddy kept going straight back in, and eventually he mastered the creature. Typically, he then relaxed, stood back, hands on hips, and grinned. 'See?' he said. 'It's easy when you know how!'

There are two distinct species of camels: the two-humped Bactrian camel of Central Asia and the one-humped dromedary of India and the Middle East. Only a few Bactrians were ever imported into Australia, but thousands of dromedaries were brought out for use in the continent's arid regions, and a strain developed which camel experts contend is equal to the very best Indian types. Just as horsemen will never agree which breed of horse is the best all-rounder, so camel men will argue as to which is the most superior dromedary. Most breeds have their supporters, but not all: everyone agrees about Dogla and Thal camels. Of these, one expert simply said, 'The Dogla is a mongrel camel, but the Thal is the most miserable of all camels.' Larrikin was behaving like a Dogla–Thal cross that day.

The Loss of a Camel

We had lost too much time to sit around over breakfast, so we set off, stiff and sore from the morning's exertions. A fierce wind sprang up from the west, flinging dust and sand in our faces. It was an effort to walk, leaning into the bitterly cold wind. Our gloves and big woolly bluey coats kept us warm, and balaclavas covered our mouths, noses and ears, but we still felt the sting of the sand as the wind blew in our faces.

The camels seemed to handle the conditions reasonably well. Their winter wool kept them warm, and in fact they were pretty well designed for this type of weather. Camels' nostrils are not round like a horse's, but are long narrow slits full of hair so that they can breathe in a sandstorm without getting a nose full of sand. Their ears, too, are small and full of hair.

The wind kept up, swirling around us as we stopped to eat on top of a large bluff, blowing sand into our lunch of dates, dried figs—which I had brought along as a special treat—and damper. A few miles after lunch brought a welcome change, for we left the stone behind, passing onto lush, well-grassed clayflats,

▲ Millions of years of life in the world's arid regions have caused the camel to evolve with narrow nostrils and ears full of hair to keep out the sand.

Birdsville looks too small to warrant a mention on the Australian map, but as the only town for 100 miles in any direction, it is of vital importance to the inhabitants of remote outback stations.

with a tall dune every few miles. The going was good and the wind had now dropped, so we decided to push on to Birdsville which, by my calculations, was only ten or eleven miles away.

Late in the afternoon, however, Larrikin abruptly sat down and refused to budge. We had already grown very concerned about him, as his condition had deteriorated markedly. We gave him a couple of injections which he accepted without comment—a bad sign in itself. His load was taken off and packed onto the others. By (reluctantly) emptying out most of the water in Walloper's tanks we lightened him enough to take half the burden; the rest went onto Ginger, which meant one less riding camel. Half an hour later, Larrikin got up and wandered off browsing as if nothing had happened, so we decided he was fit to go on.

For an hour all went well, the train moving like clockwork, then suddenly Larrikin fell over. Walloper, who at one stage had been trained to pull a wagon, simply kept going, towing the poor animal along behind him. Before I had time to halt the team Paddy did an aerial dismount and cut Larrikin's lead rope. He lay quite still for what seemed ages, then slowly righted himself into the kneeling position. He could go no further; the stony desert had taken its toll. We were only six miles short of Birdsville, in a broad valley with the Diamantina plain to the north; food and water were plentiful. But as Larrikin was unlikely to leave this area, we decided to push on, intending to come back for him in a day or two.

By now it was after five and almost dark as Paddy and I together led the team. We were both dog-tired and just kept walking, lost in our own thoughts. I have no doubt that Paddy, like me, was thinking of Larrikin back there. Would he be all right? Should we have selected him for the trip? Should I have given him some other drug, or given it to him earlier? Had he been trying to tell us this morning that he could not go on? Each of us kept his doubts and feelings quiet and kept on walking.

As the sun finally set we dropped the pace back a little, both for the camels' sakes and our own, but the camels were reluctant to alter the pace they were used to, and kept bumping into us in the dark. Chilbi and Frankie joined us, walking to take the weight off their camels. Perhaps it was due to the events we had shared that day, or a sensation common to any group walking together in the dark, but that was the first time I felt that we were a team, belonging together.

From the top of a particularly high dune the western sky spread before us sprinkled with stars, and off on the horizon, slightly to the north, twinkled the tiny cluster of lights we sought: Birdsville. Two hours later we wearily unloaded the camels by moonlight beside a shallow pool just south of the village.

▲ The pub at Birdsville, here seen temporarily without its roof, was a longed-for haven for the hot and thirsty team.

Birdsville was civilisation's last outpost, the end of the line, and the reasons for its continued existence were unclear. It consisted of a pub, a tin hall, a school, a shop, a police station and a Catholic mission. The dusty main street was wide enough for a wagon team of twenty bullocks to turn round in, and I would not blame them if they did just that.

It was a strange sensation to walk into the old stone pub after nearly 300 miles of solitude. Birdsville might be the end of the line, but its pub was an Australian legend. Built originally as a mission, a wide corrugated-iron verandah was added some years later to cut down the heat and glare from the surrounding desert. It had been the scene of many exciting and totally fictitious fights, drinking contests and devious card games in which horses, cattle stations and even wives had reportedly changed hands.

Everyone in the pub seemed to be talking at once, very loudly. Perhaps it was just in contrast to the silence of the desert, or perhaps they were all a bit drunk, as it was Friday night, but in any event it was a grand feeling to sit on a stool and take that first long, cool swig, knowing that we could fairly claim another rest day for the morrow.

Night thoughts

Back at our camp that night I lay awake wondering exactly what Burke and Wills's route through this area had been. There had been several maps published in historical books showing where they left the Diamantina River. Some showed them leaving it near Birdsville, some fifty miles south of Birdsville and others thirty miles to the east, near the bluff on which we had eaten sandy figs. Which was the actual route?

Throughout western Queensland there were a number of 'Burke and Wills trees', some with both names carved on them, others with only the initials B–W; many of them clearly showed dates and camp numbers, while others were almost indecipherable. Unfortunately, far from helping to pinpoint the path of the explorers, the vast majority were fakes. No doubt some were carved in good faith, by people wanting to mark the position of a guessed or legendary camp, but others were simply the work of pranksters. So to avoid confusion we put no faith in any of them.

While each camp's latitude and longitude were shown on various maps, these had to be speculative since Wills's journal usually mentioned the latitude only. Our best bet was to try, in combination with the latitude reading, to reconstruct Burke's route from the appearance of the countryside as it was described in the expedition's journals.

Wills's entry for the day they left the Diamantina River read:

> LAT. S. 25½° to 23¾° Camp LXXVIII to LXXXV. Sunday, December 30, 1860: Finding that the creek was trending considerably towards the east without much likelihood of altering its course, we struck off from it, taking ten days' supply of water, as there were ranges visible to the north, which had the appearance of being stony. A northeast by north course was first taken for about seven miles in order to avoid them.

Thus I was looking for a spot 25½° south of the Equator, on a large creek, which lower down ran north–south but turned to the east at this latitude, about seven miles south of a stony range. Birdsville had Mount Lewis about seven miles to the north and more ranges to the northeast, and the Diamantina River did turn here, but it was almost thirty miles too far south.

Another possible site, therefore, to the east of my sandy-fig bluff, appeared promising. It was on the Diamantina River, only a little south of 25½°S. But as we had sat there, flicking ants off our lunch, we had seen no mountains to the north, and no easterly bend in the river. That was not the site either.

Going back to the diary, I thought about our own day's routine, sitting around at night writing up the day's events, taking the star sightings. The answer, when I saw it, was obvious. Wills's diary covered that day's going, but was written at night and so gave that night's latitude. Thus they had left the creek that morning, a day's march south of 25½°. Birdsville was twenty-eight miles south of that latitude, a good day's march over alluvial earthy plain. So we were actually back on Burke's trail, and virtually on schedule, but down one camel.

Break at Birdsville

Unfortunately the schedule soon went awry again, as we realised that the camels were so tired we would need to rest them for another few days at Birdsville.

The first morning was busy with Frankie doing the weekly washing-up and Chilbi and Paddy cutting the bullock hide into strips for hobbles. I was trying to re-pack all the stores in case we needed to continue with one camel less. The town's population of about sixty people and two million crows were all equally curious about our camp beside the muddy billabong. Our work was not made any easier by the sightseers wanting us to stop and chat or wanting a ride on the camels, so we decided to hobble the camels and let them graze down the creek a bit. But when Frankie tried to find them that afternoon they had vanished. On a stony riverflat like that it was nearly impossible to track camels, so the four of us separated and went in search of them, Paddy and I going upriver and the Aborigines downstream. After an hour or so of fruitless searching even Paddy lost heart.

'The bloody flies have probably eaten them,' he said, and we returned to camp. It was a disaster: I had left the pack bags open. In our absence the crows had descended in droves and torn to pieces anything they could get hold of— toilet paper, salted bacon, tea, curry powder and, worst of all, our navigation charts, which now were shredded and strewn over the whole clearing. They had even eaten a packet of very potent chilli powder, which I hope taught them something. The loss of the navigation tables was a real disaster, for without them the sextant and computer would be useless.

At least, to cheer us up, Chilbi and Frankie returned about then with the camels. Following a big stew of crows' leftovers we headed over to town to see the weekly picture show, which was projected onto a screen beside the road with

Outback cinema-goers may never know the comforts of the big multiscreen complexes in the city, but rough-and-ready set-ups like these have a certain charm of their own. ▼

the viewers sitting in the dust and (the adult viewers at least) passing bottles of port around. The set-up was reasonably typical of remote outback cinemas, and the film was a badly dubbed Italian Western. I am not sure whether to blame the port or the scriptwriter but it was incomprehensible. This did not deter the audience, mostly Aboriginal children, who enjoyed it immensely.

The next day Paddy and Chilbi set out for the valley where Larrikin had been abandoned, and Frankie and I pottered about the camp cleaning up and attending to hundreds of tedious little chores. The day was hot and still, flies buzzed incessantly and crows circled overhead. I squatted on the muddy bank of the billabong, washing socks that had not been off my feet since Cordillo. They were so bad that Frankie, who had come over to do his washing, moved quietly further down the bank! The offending garments were hung on the nearby lignum bushes to dry, or as Paddy would say, 'for the flies to pick 'em clean'.

But when Paddy returned with Chilbi, he was in no mood for jest: they had not been able to find Larrikin, so we were definitely one camel down. At least we knew that he was up and about, for circling hawks and crows soon let you know if there was a dead animal in the area. We consoled ourselves with the thought that he could quite well live on in the wild, and die eventually of ripe old age—camels face no natural predators in Australia, other than Man.

▲ An Aboriginal woman shows off her superb damper. The art of making this staple bread eluded the author!

We had supper that night with the sisters at the local mission, a delightful alternative to my cooking. The sisters may have had the saving of souls as their primary concern, but more pragmatically they ran a clinic and operated the radio link for the flying-doctor service, which was vital for all outlying cattle stations, mining camps and long-distance truck drivers. As our contribution to the evening's meal we took along one of Chilbi's dampers. Damper was a sore point with me. I prided myself on being a reasonable camp cook, but damper utterly defeated me. Chilbi, on the other hand, turned out beautiful golden loaves every time. I would sit by the campfire and watch his every move, trying to find the secret. He kneaded the dough carefully, tossed in rough amounts of salt and baking soda, threw a shovelful of coals into a pit, put the camp oven loaded with the dough into the pit, threw earth over it and walked away. Then he would lie back and light up his pipe, totally unconcerned. Later on, at just the right moment (he didn't have a watch) he would wander over and dig up a perfectly cooked, nicely risen damper. I fear that to my dying day I will be turning out dampers that are quite flat, black outside and soggy inside. We had an unspoken understanding that I was to stay away from dampers and concentrate on stews.

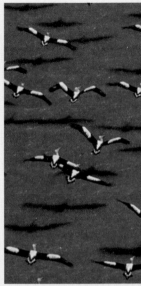

A male emu stands guard over a clutch of beautiful dark green eggs. As in so many other respects, emus are oddities when it comes to nesting. The female plays no part in incubating the eggs—nor in rearing the chicks either.

Birdlife Down Under

AUSTRALIA, with over 700 bird species, is a birdwatcher's paradise. Many are not only unique to the country, like the laughing kookaburra with its raucous cackle, but also highly distinctive—and none more so than the flightless emu, which lays up to 20 dark green eggs, stands six feet tall and is able to run at 30 miles an hour.

And in this land of surprises for the unwary, what could be more appropriate than black swans? These beautiful creatures share inland waters with pelicans, which fly in great flocks to their favourite fishing grounds, where they swim in formation and drive the fish into the shallows from where they can be easily scooped out.

Australia is home to no less than 50 species of parrot, including pink and grey galahs, whose noisy congregations bring the normally quiet desert to life. Parrots, like many Australian birds, are nomadic rather than migratory: they

pursue food and water whenever and wherever these can be found, rather than travelling to a set destination at specific times of year.

Song birds account for a further 300 species, some just as colourful as their talkative counterparts. Among the prettiest is the Gouldian finch, whose plumage incorporates almost all the colours of the rainbow. Sadly the finch's very attractiveness has made it a popular caged bird, and extensive trapping for this trade has drastically reduced its numbers in the wild.

More fortunate is the huge wedge-tailed eagle, the country's largest bird of prey with an eight-foot wingspan. For many years the wedge-tailed eagle was suspected of killing lambs, and was therefore widely hunted. However, when it was proved, that the eagle's preferred live prey was in fact rabbit, and that otherwise it often ate carrion, laws were introduced to protect it.

▲ The laughing kookaburra is the largest member of the kingfisher family, but paradoxically rarely eats fish, preferring instead to eat insects, reptiles and rodents.

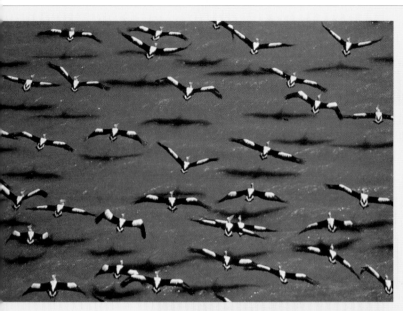

▲ The black-and-white plumage of pelicans creates a striking mosaic as they survey their fishing grounds, their shadows presaging doom for the fish below.

Wedge-tailed eagles rarely use their deadly beaks against lambs, as was once thought. Those they do take are usually dead or dying already. ▶

▲ A bare tree has acquired a distinctive pink and grey foliage in the form of galahs, which gather in flocks of up to a thousand to forage for seeds.

The discovery of this bird came as a shock to early British visitors to Australia, who had long used the term 'black swan' to describe an impossibility. ▼

▲ The red-headed Gouldian finch, one of Australia's most dramatically-coloured finches, is now comparatively rare.

CHAPTER 4

Channel Country

MEN AND CAMELS SEEMED TO HAVE RECOVERED after our pleasant break and it was time to hit the road. We were up at dawn, but the camels had wandered miles down the river again, and by the time we had saddled up and filled the water tanks it was quite late.

The ground was bare and hard, with the sand dunes of the Simpson Desert visible to the west and low rocky ranges ahead and to the east. Although the winds add to them in some years, and erode them away in others, the dunes in this part of the world are quite stable and are thought to be about 7,000 years old. In the centre the sand had been packed into a core, which made them fairly solid. They supported quite a variety of bushes and shrubs whose greens and olives contrasted nicely with the red sand of the dunes, while the grassy clay flats in between supported a unique fauna of small birds, reptiles and mammals.

We were back into our pace now, a gentle rhythm which was almost hypnotic. The timeless quality of the surrounding countryside somehow enhanced this effect: there was no clue as to what century it was, where you were, or who else, if anyone, might have been there before you.

It was a rude intrusion therefore when an old Toyota utility truck roared up behind us in a cloud of dust and fumes. The driver was a stranger to us, and introduced himself as Ken-from-the-Curry before telling me that there was an important call from Sydney for me on the radio-telephone back at Birdsville. We were by now about ten miles out so he offered, as people do in these parts, to run me in and bring me back out. As we climbed on board he handed me a can of beer along with an apology because it wasn't too cold. (It was, in fact, just short of boiling.) My heart was in my mouth as we returned, partly because of Ken's driving but mainly because of this phone call. I felt instinctively, as any father does, that something terrible had happened to one of the kids.

To make matters worse, when we arrived the radio-telephone was closed down for lunch, and by the time it reopened an hour later, the Sydney 'party'

Few remote areas in Australia have telephone lines, so the airwaves are used instead to send and receive messages via radio-telephone. ▼

was out to lunch. After much fretting and worrying on my part the Sydney party came on the air, and turned out just to be a journalist wanting to know how we were doing. I told him in simple, clear, camel-driver's language.

Ken-from-the-Curry had not been able to wait any longer and thus I had to accept any lift I could get—in the event a pair of extremely drunk holidaymakers. They drove so fast that it was difficult to see the camel tracks in the fading light. We drove around aimlessly for a while and it was quite dark before we spotted a tiny twinkle of campfire about half a mile to the west. The team had made twenty miles that day despite the late start. The gibber had been so bad that Paddy had had to walk nearly all the way and in my absence Frankie had walked beside him for a good way as well. They were dog-tired, and I issued them with a double ration of bacon which I cooked as fast as I could—by the look of them they would have eaten it raw.

My holidaymaker friends decided that this camp life suited them, so they pitched tent nearby and infuriated us all by talking 'black-fella' talk to the Aborigines, which sounded like gibberish (with a soft 'g') from the Italian Western we had watched

It was the welcoming glow from a campfire that enabled the author to find his fellow travellers as night fell over the outback.

recently. It was degrading to hear this condescending nonsense, and I was about to say something when I caught a glance from Chilbi and noticed the twinkle in his eye. It was all the old man could do to stop himself laughing, but in his most solemn manner he produced halting words of utter rubbish which fooled them completely, and so perfectly did he lead them on that I had to retire behind a lignum bush where I found Paddy already rolling in stitches of silent laughter, tears running down his face. The incident became one of the high-lights of our trip.

We returned to the camp to find that one of our guests had fallen into the fire and burnt his hand while the other had trodden on our frying pan and broken it. It was a relief to see them depart the next day.

In the morning Paddy told me that Frances had a bad sore on her hipbone—the extra weight in her packs since the loss of Larrikin had worn the skin badly, so the load was shifted onto Cleo, who had until then been lightly loaded.

We had been camped on the edge of a fairly extensive marsh, and lost quite a bit of time getting out of it and back onto the plain. This marsh, luckily, was dry, but they could persist for several years after a big flood, and sometimes a thin dry crust formed over them, under which there was a quagmire. The best way to find out if this had happened was to let your companion go first.

The going that day was good for the first twelve miles or so—flat, even clay with little vegetation beyond scattered tussocks of dead grass, and the occasional mulga or myall tree. We lunched under one of these—damper, dates and biltong again—but lunch over, we had gone only a short way before the good going gave way to barren stony downs. Far off on the western horizon a low bleak range was barely visible in the heat haze, and to the east the desert stretched unbroken as far as the eye could see.

The region we were now going through is called the Channel Country: a vast desert claypan intersected by a network of river channels up to twenty miles wide which drain the area after rainfall but which at other times can be completely dry. The channels are marked by grasslands with timber lines along the main courseways. This southwestern area of Queensland is very dry, and when there is water in these channels it has usually come from heavy rainfalls far to the north and east, which may not occur for years on end. About 20,000 years ago, before the sand dunes formed, the now dry areas were apparently much better watered, as fossils of giant marsh-dwelling kangaroos, turtles and even crocodiles have been found there.

Back in Sydney after the expedition I took Chilbi to a museum, where I showed him the skeleton of an extinct *Diprotodon* (a giant wombat) from his tribal area. He just stared and shook his head. He could not conceive of the land

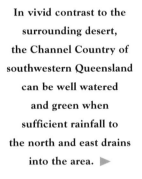

In vivid contrast to the surrounding desert, the Channel Country of southwestern Queensland can be well watered and green when sufficient rainfall to the north and east drains into the area. ▶

so familiar to him ever having been any different, ever having been populated with such strange, monstrous creatures as this. It was almost equally difficult for me, walking through the Channel Country that particular day, to conceive of it as a lush marshland. But the terrain was improving a little as we went, until evening brought us to our destination—the ruins of Cacoory homestead, its old stone walls painted crimson by the rays of the sun as it set across the desert.

Kangaroo Country

We set camp that night at the nearby waterhole, sweet and cool beneath the shading coolabahs. Frankie was relieved of camp duties and sent to catch us a big fat fish, a task he undertook willingly. Fish in these waterholes, like freshwater shrimps, proliferated rapidly after floods, their embryos, dormant in the hard clay above the waterline, hatching as soon as the water rose and the clay softened. Unfortunately, that day Frankie had no success and we ate biltong stew yet again. At least our biltong was made from beef; Burke made his from horsemeat.

The last torch packed up that night, so the journals and navigation log (prepared now by dead reckoning, with our estimates of each hour's march related to compass readings and the map) had to be written by firelight, the glow of which lit up the coolabahs overhead to create a scene as snug and warm as any living room. As we sat around the dying embers sharing a late night billy, the talk turned to what the Aborigines called min min lights, which haunted this region. I had been given a first-hand account of this phenomenon by a stockman I met at Birdsville. The event took place not ten miles southeast of this waterhole, and he told the story like this:

> 'Bout five year ago, we was bringin' a mob of bullock from Sandringham down to Durrie. We were havin' a hell of a time shiftin' 'em, they were so bloody poor you could smell their guts through their ribs. Anyhow, we were about ten stragglers down this day so I rode back on me own to pick 'em up. Took me all day to find 'em, and by nightfall I was still a long way out. It woulda been about ten mile south o' Cacoory when I see this light like a car 'eadlight comin' at me. It pulled up about fifty yard short, and then just moved along beside us for a while. Well I rode over and got about twenty yard short o' the bloody thing when it took off, straight past the bullocks so o' course they go in every bloody direction. I let 'em go and head for home, but this bloody light comes back and keeps along level with me, even pulls up when I open a gate, or shoots around in front of me at a hundred mile an hour. I was only half a mile short o' camp when it disappeared. Never 'eard any sound, but I can tell yer that horse o' mine saw it too, he was twitchy as hell and shakin' all over. Only time I ever seen it, but the blokes from over Muncoonie way reckon they seen 'em lots o' times, and I believe 'em too.'

I think he did, too: he was a leathery, down-to-earth sort of a character, and only mildly intoxicated at the time.

▲ 'You are in the land of the min min light', proclaims a roadside notice in a Channel Country town. No satisfactory explanation of the source of these eerie bright lights has ever been found.

There had been many such sightings of min min lights in this area, by all sorts of people, both black and white, and somehow they were difficult to explain away as incandescent marsh gas or hallucinations. Paddy summed up the situation. 'Any of you blokes see a bloody min min,' he said as he rolled into his swag, 'I reckon you better grab it and shove it in the torch. Then if it works we can bloody patent it.'

During the night a strong wind came up and the whistling and rustling of the trees woke me. Somewhere quite nearby a small animal was shuffling about, audible in the brief quiet spells between wind gusts. I dozed off again, making a mental note to check for tracks next morning. They were difficult to spot in that hard ground, but Frankie picked them up. The tracks were more abundant near a rocky outcrop about half a mile south of the camp, where a number of small, rabbit-style burrows had been dug. They showed that the animal had a long hind foot and a hand-shaped forepaw. It could have been a bilby, a small, rare, desert-dwelling marsupial, but we could not wait around to catch one for a photograph. One of the great frustrations of the trip was not having enough time to pull up and explore the wildlife around us.

But on we pressed, last night's snug camp forgotten already as a barren, tree-less plain unfolded in front of us. It was the hottest day yet; both Paddy and I were stripped to the waist by morning break. As he walked along in the lead, hands on hips, head down, I noticed that he was getting quite a tan. But as the sun rose higher and the sweat started to trickle down his back, quite a lot of his tan ran down with it. None of us had really noticed it, but we had had only one shower in over 300 miles.

As we came up over a ridge Chilbi let out an excited yell, 'Marloo! Marloo!' This meant nothing to me, but looking in the direction he was pointing, I could just make out the shape of a kangaroo far off to our right; 'marloo' was obviously an Aboriginal name for it. Paddy grabbed the rifle and, crouched double, ran quietly down a shallow gully, coming up to within fifty yards of the roo, and despatching it quickly. Fresh meat!

While Paddy had been stalking it the roo had moved a little, and something about the way it moved seemed odd to me, so I walked over with Nugget and the tucker bag to check it. On inspecting it I got quite a shock: it was not a kangaroo at all but a large wallaby, with a head and body length of about three and a half feet, and a red head and neck. There were not supposed to be any wallabies in that area—they are typically creatures of thick scrub or mountainsides rather than of open plains and grasslands—and if this was a red-necked wallaby, as I think it was, then it was at least 500 miles too far inland. Our luggage problem was such that we carried no preservatives, so we could take back no specimens for firm identification. Instead, we cut off both hind legs and tail, put them in a bag on top of Walloper, had a small sip of water each, and headed off once more, all thinking of meat—fried, grilled or boiled—just fresh meat.

It is strange how necessity can change a person. My last trip to the outback had been to rescue orphaned joeys (young kangaroos) and I had spent sleepless nights trying to wean the young animals onto a bottle; now I was drooling over the thought of eating one. It struck me that perhaps all the trappings of 'civilised' man are nothing more than a thin veneer which simply falls away when faced with any primitive drive such as hunger.

On Burke and Wills's return journey, when they were already showing signs of fatigue, Wills was to record the passing of a camel with the simple epitaph 'Feasting Camp'. And so we pressed on, determined to make our twenty-five miles before we pitched our own Feasting Camp.

Idyll at Koolivoo

By midafternoon it was still fiercely hot on the barren plains, and the heat haze and mirages had become worse than ever before. At the changeover, as we both sat resting our backs against the lead camel, Paddy and I shared a cigarette. We generally said little on such occasions as there was little to say. Paddy's eyes were red slits in a face smeared with dust and sweat, but as he got up to take the lead-rope he peered intently out towards the west.

'I don't know what you think, mate, but either I'm going blind or that bloody mirage there's real.'

A glance in the direction Paddy was looking showed a vast lake, stretching for miles, that had to be a mirage. But after an hour's going it was still there, and seemed to stretch straight across our path. It had me wondering now, so I pulled out the map and did a few quick calculations.

We had started at 8.15am, and had lost half an hour stalking and skinning the roo, and half an hour for lunch. Thus we had been going for six-and-a-half hours, and had therefore come about nineteen or twenty miles north from Cacoory. The map of that region did show two gigantic lakes ahead, one some miles to our left and the other far away on our right, but we had expected them

◄ The still waters that appear to reflect trees and sky in this desert scene do not exist: they are a mirage, which occurs where hot air near the ground meets denser, cooler air above it. Light passing through these temperature zones bends to produce an image below the horizon.

to be dry. They were linked on the map by a stream labelled Koolivoo, which seemed to run across our path about three miles ahead.

I was not yet entirely convinced (we had camped on the dry beds of a couple of 'lakes' already) but slowly it became clear that we were indeed approaching some sort of watercourse, for the countryside was changing with each step, and a profusion of wild flowers, lignum and verbena closed in around us. Since cutting north from the Diamantina River we had been following Burke's route fairly closely. In 1861 this region was a far cry from the oasis we found, for it was then bone dry. We pushed through the lush undergrowth to a fast-flowing stream, its banks lined with river red gums and thick tangled lignum bush. The noise of our arrival set off a massed flutter of wings as hundreds and hundreds of waterfowl—ducks, teals, herons, ibises, cormorants and pelicans—took to the air. Nearby on the river flat a herd of fat Herefords grazed contentedly, barely pausing to watch us pass. Butterflies hovered over the golden flowers, and flocks of finches and silver-eyes flitted from bush to bush heralding our arrival.

We had not quite made our daily target of miles yet, but a spot such as this was too good to miss, so we made camp on an island in a large shallow pool to one

Rivers in the outback engender a total transformation in the landscape. Barren plains give way to burgeoning riverbanks, supporting varied wildlife and plants as large as these majestic river red gums. ▼

side of the fast-moving river. The water was fairly clear, and the large number of pelicans paddling majestically along it indicated an abundance of fish.

Chilbi relieved me of cooking duties, as the 'marloo' Paddy had shot was one of his specialities and so, while Frankie tried unsuccessfully again for big fat fish, I wandered downstream for a bath. The water was freezing cold and bracing, and to climb into clean clothes smelling of soap was a sensuous delight.

During this operation I was subject to the inquisitive stares of a large rookery of spoonbills, and was honked at by a passing pink-eared duck with her brood. After the desert, Koolivoo was the most idyllic oasis one could hope for, and the smell of roasting meat back at camp was tantalising. With Paddy out after duck and Frankie fishing, we had expectations of even better things to come, but were none too upset when we finally had to make do with what we had. It was delicious, and when we were all so full we could eat no more, we still had the marloo's tail left to have cold for lunch the next day.

Tension in the Team

The dawn chorus of the waterfowl at Koolivoo woke us next morning and for a while we lay in our swags watching the flocks circling, banking and skimming the surface of the waterhole.

Finally we dragged ourselves out and were just getting dressed when a flock of ducks swam past not thirty feet from where I stood. By the time I had the rifle loaded they

had moved off a bit, but I managed to hit one, and thought I hit another, for it limped along upstream. I have a deep loathing of anything wounded being left to suffer and so I raced up along the bank, stumbling and falling through thick lignum scrub without a stitch on, the wounded bird keeping just ahead all the way. Finally I reached the end of the island on which we were camped and had to dive in after it. The water was freezing, and on surfacing I saw the bird double back the way it had come. Paddy joined the chase by diving in ahead of it, whereupon it took off quite happily, not wounded at all, leaving us both to return to camp, naked and wet, and blue with cold. We were greeted with a cup of tea and many derisive remarks by the others.

We warmed up after breakfast when we started the day's march, the circulation slowly returning to fingers and toes. It was a beautiful morning as we moved across the valley, through mile after mile of green meadow sprinkled with golden flowers, and we noticed a number of little black-and-gold birds which I have not seen before or since. We saw our first bustard or plains turkey as well. They are good-sized birds and supposed to be excellent eating, but are protected. They were very wary of us and as soon as they saw us coming they moved well out of rifle-range and temptation's way.

Various people I later spoke to in those parts told me that although you could not get near these birds on horseback or on foot they could for some reason be

▲ The aptly named royal spoonbill uses its peculiar bill to sweep the water in search of fish or crustaceans, crushing the latter with protruding knobs at the bill's base.

approached easily by car. I asked one character up north if he realised that they were protected. 'The only ones protected up here, mate,' he said, 'are the ones with a Wildlife Ranger in front of 'em.'

We were to encounter the bustard a lot from here on, so that although their numbers had been severely reduced at one stage, they seemed to be making a comeback in these parts. Evidently not everyone shared that man's outlook.

We were back on the barren downs again by lunchtime, and pulled up under a solitary stunted eucalyptus. Out came the cups, water bags, dried dates and damper, but no kangaroo tail. 'Where's the bloody roo tail?' I asked. There were quick, embarrassed glances exchanged, then Chilbi spoke up: he had eaten it as we rode along that morning. I had some sharp words to say on the subject of sharing, and our lunch of damper and dates was finished in a heavy silence.

I was readjusting one of the packs on Cleo just before we remounted when Chilbi came and asked what was the name of the next settlement. 'Bedourie,' I said.

'Well, boss, I think I better finish up there,' he said. Paddy came over, and between us we managed to convince him that his antisocial act was not that important, just as long as it didn't happen again.

Things calmed down, but it was now an uneasy camp; a division had fallen between black and white. Although it was a trivial incident, it had served to bring to the surface feelings which had built up gradually over the trip. I had come to prove a point, and I knew what I was in for; Paddy had, I believe, come initially out of a sense of duty to his brother Greg, but, once committed, he had thrown himself into things completely, accepting the trip as a challenge and an adventure. We two had shared all the walking and much of the camp work between us. If two men on their own split the work in half, all was well, but if two others looked on, then possibilities for resentment cropped up.

▲ All 20 species of bustard that exist worldwide have suffered severe decline in the last century. Some have lost their habitat to pasture, some have fallen prey to foxes, others have wound up on dinner plates. This Australian species, the kori bustard, or plains turkey, is now protected by law.

Why had the Aborigines agreed to come? Communicating complex matters of motivation was beyond the capacity of our limited shared language. Chilbi, since he was getting very little pay, had probably come partly to get away from the routine of mission life, partly to break in young Frankie, who was on the threshold of manhood, and partly because he too had been a friend of Greg's. Frankie was there probably because his father had said so. Both lacked any motivation to do the trip the way we were doing it. So resentment was out of place on our part, and guilt on theirs. It was a situation that needed time to work itself out.

We marched in silence all afternoon, our track winding up over high dunes or running along in the gullies between them. Finally nightfall came when we were still in dune country, miles from any surface water, so we camped on the side of a large sand hill. The long walk had eased the tension a little, and everyone got a good and equal share of roast duck to show that there were no hard feelings.

Later I lay awake, staring up at the stars and wondering about us and about the Aboriginal peoples generally. It seemed to me that our cultures were bewilderingly far apart. My European outlook had developed in a fertile environment where the crops grown in spring and summer had to be harvested and stored for use over the cold winter. Our culture therefore was based on the principle of 'he who works hardest plants more, harvests more, stores more, so he and his family will live better in the next winter'. Thus, as Paddy and I did, Europeans threw themselves into things in order to produce enough to eat tomorrow and to store up some food for the day after. (Just like the roo tail.)

But the Pitjantjatjara faced different problems, for their world was hot, dry and barren, and there were few plants which could be harvested in large enough quantities to put much aside for tomorrow. Australian animals were small and few in number, and meat did not keep well in this climate. Thus the Aborigines had developed a culture suitable to a barren land, getting just enough for today, then saving their energy. Any excess work would waste precious energy and sweat, both energy and water being scarce commodities. Storage was pointless, since when the waterhole dried up, the tribe had to move on, carrying everything with them.

Had our culture evolved in this country, it would have been very similar to theirs, and our outlook, on a venture like this, would no doubt have been similar. It was upsetting, however, that in our party the two peoples—each acting true to their values—had been thrown into conflict.

I tossed and turned and finally, giving up sleep, sat up and stirred the fire for another billy as I mulled over Burke's experiences. One of his main flaws had

▲ **One of the great lessons the author learned on his expedition was a greater understanding of Aboriginal culture, one based on adaptation to a harsh environment.**

been his inability to manage men. His foreman, Charles Ferguson, was sacked at Menindee, and both George Landells, his second-in-charge and camel expert, and Dr Beckler resigned at that time.

I looked across the fire at Paddy, our camel man, and wondered what he thought of my man-management today, and of the treatment Chilbi and Frankie had received from us. Both were now curled up together right next to the fire, as was their people's way. Could they understand the clash of the two cultures, or did they simply see me as a mad leader who got angry over perfectly normal and harmless things?

Off to the west somewhere a dingo called, making me feel very lonely hunched by myself on the side of the dune. I thought of home and of the family sitting round the fire—but they would all be snug in bed by now. The thought of snug beds made me realise how cold it had become. I rolled into my swag and dozed off, thinking of the kids and watching Achernar, one of the brightest stars in the southern sky, sinking towards the horizon.

The Tension Eases

Before too long it was the start of another day and with it the start of a new regimen. Frankie had the fire going and the camp all shipshape; Chilbi had the camels back from their night's grazing, and they were already half packed when

The moon sinks and the sun rises to reveal the tracks of night-time wanderers—in this case dingoes and, with long, narrow lines, beetles. ▼

I awoke. It seemed I had not been sitting alone last night: Chilbi showed me the tracks of a big dingo, pointing out the spot not twenty feet away where he had crouched watching me, then the tracks where he came right into camp, probably soon after I hit the swag.

As I peered at the tracks in the sand to try to figure out how Chilbi could tell their age, I noticed something of even greater interest—the silver wrapper from a powerful pain-killing anti-arthritic drug, unlike anything I carried. It emerged that Chilbi had seriously hurt his right knee in a fall from a horse several years ago and that the injury was being badly aggravated by the trip. The sisters at Birdsville had given him tablets on the advice of the flying doctor; Chilbi had not wanted to worry me about it.

With me feeling like an insensitive martinet, we set off across a wide plain of wild flowers, a solid mass of gold. The soil was of a rich, black, loamy texture cracked into wide fissures by the scorching heat. We passed the carcass of a cow which the dingoes had killed while she was calving. A thousand crows were now feasting unconcerned by our passing. One of the first things a stranger was likely to notice out here was the lack of odours: no exhaust fumes, perfumes, gas leaks or garbage. Only the sickly sweet smell of the occasional carcass broke the monotony. We found that this lack of noises, odours or movement heightened the senses incredibly. In the city, people could live right on a main road and be completely unaware of the noise of a thousand cars, but out here they would re-tune their senses to hear a car ten miles away, or pick out the distant glint of sun on moving metal. Yet, while the senses were tuned to a high pitch by this vacuum, the brain was dulled by inactivity, and I recall feeling completely and utterly bored that day, having exhausted all conceivable thought. That evening I wrote, '...I think I have sung every song I ever knew, whistled every tune ever written.'

▲ **The bleached bones of a cow offer a stark reminder of the harsh realities of wilderness life.**

We were now living a very simple life, little more complicated than that of animals: up at dawn, walking at an even pace all day, eating whatever happened to turn up and finding a tree to sleep under when the sun went down. Such a lifestyle required no more mental activity than that of a migrating gnu, and in my opinion that was why gnus never developed any further. It was also probably why my mind was becoming less active. Odd, vague thoughts on this point or that gathered like frail clouds and then dispersed again without coming to any definite conclusions.

It was obviously the same for Paddy, whose choice of songs was, if anything, even more limited than mine.

'Gee, Paddy, you ever thought of reciting that tune at the Sydney Opera House?'

'Yep, lots of times. But I thought I'd save it for your parents' wedding.'

Perhaps we were just getting on each other's nerves in this silence. We were very tired, and the appearance of a large, stationary dust cloud low on the northern horizon failed to spur us on to any great exertion; we just kept plodding on. It turned out to be a mob of a thousand bullocks plodding equally wearily south to find new grazing land, as the country 'up the top end' was getting pretty dry.

The head drover rode over on a fine grey hack which at first looked extremely nervous of the camels. But after five minutes it was riding right beside us, even sniffing the camels, and the theory of camels spooking horses took another tumble. The drover rode with us while his men harried the slowly moving herd past us, and the talk drifted from camels to horses, from waterholes to droughts, and from saddles back to camels. There is a ritual which is gone through in any such encounter in the bush, a ritual which is as polite and formal (despite the coarse language) as any encountered at Government House. Certain topics are compulsory: your health, the weather, your destination, and whether or not you have sufficient meat and water. Any real sign of curiosity is regarded as prying, and topics such as politics, religion or current affairs are taboo.

It was amusing to listen to a stockman going through this polite litany when it was obvious that he had never seen a camel and was dying to find out all about them, but was prevented by good manners from bombarding you with questions.

He bade us farewell as we left the plain and headed through a wide channel of soft alluvial sand, which was hard going, even for the camels. Beyond this was a magnificent old dune which ran as straight as a die for five or so miles. Usually, just at the foot of a dune, on each side, there was an area of well-packed clay and soil, which, providing the dune was pointing in the right direction, was good going. This one was excellent, and we rushed along at a good rate, covering the twenty-two miles to Bedourie by 2.30pm. We set camp in a deep gully running off Eyre Creek, a mile or so south of the tiny outpost.

Desert Oasis

Bedourie consisted of a two-room pub-cum-hotel and a couple of ramshackle houses. After unloading we made our way to the hotel, stumbling through shallow gilgais (or hollows) hidden beneath the long grass. The pub seemed

▲ Clouds of russet dust herald the passage of a cattle herd on its way to new pastures.

pitch-dark after the glare of the sun, and quite cool by comparison; the steady buzz of flies and the *cra-cra* of crows outside were muted by the stone walls to a distant murmur. We were the only customers and, sensing no desire for conversation on the part of the proprietor, we contented ourselves with reading faded race-meeting posters as we sipped the lukewarm beer.

It seemed that man had not managed to do a lot with this place since Burke and Wills passed through. It had that defeated air about it, like a cow waiting to die, the sort of place where anyone with any get-up-and-go had got up and gone, leaving behind only those who could not, for whatever reason, make the break. Or perhaps it was the remoteness of the place and the harshness of the region which defeated them, for few human ventures could withstand year upon year of drought, followed by massive floods which swept down on a front many miles

◀ **The Royal Hotel at Bedourie was not, perhaps, the most regal of venues, but at least it provided shade and a beer for the weary travellers.**

wide, casting the debris of fences and dreams high up on the side of the dunes. We bought a bottle of beer each and wandered back to camp to treat the camels before nightfall.

Frances still had a bad pack sore over the point of her hipbone, which had developed into an abscess beneath the thick woolly fleece. She was not at all cooperative when being treated, in contrast to Walloper who sat quietly as I treated a pack gall over his rib cage where the back of the water tank had been rubbing.

Remedies for these pack galls were as many and varied as cures for the common cold. Bedouin tribes rubbed a mixture of camel urine and pigeon manure into them, but as pigeons were not always available I had brought an alternative cure. An Afghan from Alice Springs who was over eighty years old

Flames from a campfire
illuminate the branches
of a tree against a dark,
clear night sky. ▷

had once given me a recipe for treating pack galls: a mixture of sulphate of zinc and lead acetate, which apparently dated back to the time of the Pharaohs, prompting us to nickname it Pharaoh's Brew. Surely though, I had thought, there must be something more advanced than that. I checked with John Keep, Professor of Veterinary Medicine at Sydney University, who laughed when he heard this.

'That's almost the exact recipe for white lotion,' he said. 'Used a lot of it on the army remounts during the war. Good stuff it is, too. Most human skin lotions in use today are based on it—zinc creams and calamine lotions for instance.'

So the Pharaohs were spot on, and Pharaoh's Brew was what we used.

As the next R-and-R day (for Rest and Repairs) was due on the morrow, we were to have a big treat for dinner that night with bacon, dried peas and beer. The bacon was by now covered in green mould and smelling decidedly off, but it was still possible to eat the inner parts. Even after a thorough cooking, however, the inside bacon still tasted mouldy, and it was lucky that the warmish beer rinsed out the rancid aftertaste. It was a cold night and the sky was so clear that even the dimmest stars were visible. A breeze sprang up just before we turned in, dropping the temperature several degrees. Since we were camped in long dry grass we could risk only the smallest of fires, and we spent a restless, chilly night.

We were trailing days behind Burke's headlong pace now, a fact that preyed on my mind. It was tempting to push the camels just five or six miles farther each night, or to omit our regular rest days, but I resisted both ideas. The veterinary manuals of the British Indian Army could not be lightly ignored, and they emphasised that, ideally, camels should be marched for twenty miles a day (our present average) at most. As for rest days, the camel patrols in service today in the armies of India, Egypt and the Sudan are all rested thoroughly after each five-to-seven day period of duty. So Burke was out of step with more experienced camel men. The question in my mind was, 'Do I copy Burke's dash or their measured pace?' One way I'd lose camels, the other, historic realism.

Morning brought with it an exciting discovery. While walking up to the outpost the previous day we had noticed a grove of date palms some hundred yards to our left, but had not remarked on it. However, in the light of dawn steam could be seen rising up in the cold morning air. It was an eerie sight and we wandered over to investigate, coming to a halt on the bank of a pool—large, deep and sapphire blue, with wisps of steam rising off the surface. An enormous subterranean aquifer, the Artesian Basin, lies under much of eastern Australia, and this was obviously one of the thermal springs which derived from it. We raced back to camp and returned with towels and soap. As we dived in, the water closed over us, so soft and warm that we wanted to stay there for ever.

Frankie surfaced with a shriek of joy, his ebony face alight with glee as he dived and splashed like a playful dolphin. When he paused for air he would float for a minute or two, eyes closed and teeth gleaming in a smile of pure ecstasy. The pool was quite deep, and algae coated the bottom like a patchwork quilt. The water was crystal clear and heavy with mineral salts, the heat penetrating and soothing weary muscles, gradually relaxing the whole body and lulling the mind. It was a delightful place to float half asleep and watch the steam rise up past the date palms, but we had to make practical use of this opportunity as well, and so proceeded to wash clean the foulest collection of clothes I had ever smelled. This was followed by breakfast of bacon and several billies of tea before

the inevitable chores were allotted: a new headstall and two sets of hobbles had to be made; a pack bag had to be sewn up; the radio had to be tested; maps for the next leg must be dug out and the old ones put away (with waterholes marked for the return trip); dishes must be washed, and much, much more...

Fresh from our morning's swim we worked nonstop through the heat of the day and by midafternoon we stood back, hot and sweating, to survey the results of our labours. Satisfied, we turned our attention to treating Frances's pack sores, a task which needed all hands: one to hold her head down, two to lie on top of her and hold the leg-ropes, and one to treat the wound. She was not a good patient, our Frances—not vicious, but prone to panic. Whereas Walloper would take a long time to figure out what to do in a given situation and remain immobile while the process of thinking took place, Frances would go straight into it, generally going on the wrong side of a tree, or up the steepest part of any slope. Her saving grace was her stamina, for although she was rangy and only of medium height, she could carry a heavy load with the best of them. Still, when really bothered, she could kick with the best of them, too.

The ordeal over, we all trudged over to the Artesian spring for an afternoon dip but were sadly let down, for it was too hot to refresh sweaty men in the heat of the afternoon, and was now surrounded by clouds of hungry mosquitoes. We were hurried into getting dressed again by Chilbi muttering, '*Kwara* [women] coming'.

The Sea Beneath the Sand

W HEN THE EXPLORER Charles Sturt set out from Adelaide in 1844 at the start of his epic Central Australian Expedition, among his baggage was a most unlikely item: a small boat. For Sturt, like many others of his day, was convinced that in the centre of the continent there lay a vast inland sea. When he returned to Adelaide 17 months later, however, the boat was unused; there had been no great sea—at least, not a visible one.

What Sturt had been unaware of as he and his companions thirsted on the parched deserts was that beneath their feet lay millions upon millions of gallons of water: the Great Artesian Basin. Rainwater flowing down from the western slopes of the Great Divide

gathers underground, and is absorbed into a massive layer of porous sandstone rock to create an aquifer, or water-bearing rock; this particular aquifer—one of a number in Australia— is the largest in the world, extending for 650,000 square miles.

Every now and then, an oasis in the desert indicates a place where water from the Great Artesian Basin has forced its way to the surface. Elsewhere, people have to seek it out by drilling bores into the ground—sometimes to a depth of several thousand feet. The water from these deep bores can reach boiling point, and some homes in Queensland actually have supplies of naturally hot water piped to them.

▲ **Precious water from the Great Artesian Basin bubbles up through a bore hole and into an irrigation channel in Queensland.**

Two local Aboriginal women wandered up, accompanied by their children, and we all moved off together, leaving the mosquitoes in charge of the springs. The women treated Chilbi with great respect, as indeed nearly all Aborigines did on our trip. They obviously carried little to eat themselves and joined us in our afternoon treat of dried fruit, meat and damper, gratefully accepting some tea and cigarettes while Paddy, hot and tired though he was, gave each of the children a ride on Alice.

They came back late in the afternoon, and brought us bread and jam, which Chilbi accepted as if they had given him the Crown Jewels. They could ill afford to spare the food, but he knew it would have been very bad manners to refuse, and he also accepted their invitation to dinner.

Aboriginal Interlude

That night Paddy decided to stay in camp with Frankie, while Chilbi and I made our way across to the outpost, stumbling through the Mitchell grass and gilgais in the dark. As we entered the tiny pub this time a lively scene greeted us: at least ten people crowded the bar for the Saturday night get-together.

We were soon engaged in conversation with a couple of stockmen from one of the outlying stations who, true to form, avoided asking about our strange venture until all the preliminary remarks about the weather and so on had been thoroughly dealt with.

Chilbi went off to his supper and the crowd thinned somewhat, leaving half a dozen of us to chew the cud round the big log fire. The talk flowed back and forth; stories of broken axles followed talk of floods; good cattle dogs were topped by good stock horses; dingoes shot at 1,000 yards were bettered by ones shot at 2,000. The firelight flickered across the faces that gazed into it, each story bringing back distant memories to the other faces, either softening them into a smile or striking a sad note, the face drawing tight and closing up.

One woman recalled arriving here as a young girl sitting beside her parents in a buckboard (a crude open carriage) on the long haul up the Birdsville Track. She recounted those long-ago days wistfully, remembering how they kept the shotgun loaded as the long trains of Afghan camel teams approached. Another told of his mother, long buried, who used to go out and barter with the Afghans, while his father and brother stayed in the house, covering her with rifles. I began to realise that I had been hasty in my judgment of this place. Some of the people here were dropouts, true, but the rest were determined bushpeople who would not swap this hard life for any other and who were content to live much as the pioneers had done.

The talk drifted to the trip I was doing. The possibility that I was bloody mad was mentioned several times, and also that I was too far to the west, since the Aborigines over on Pallico Channel, fifteen-odd miles east of Bedourie, used to tell of Burke's camping there. They may have been right too, but it was hard to be definite on Burke's route through this area.

The mention of the old Pallico tribe brought up the subject of the Aborigines, obviously a hot topic in this area, and I noticed that the only person present with any Aboriginal blood in him went out and busied himself getting more firewood during the discussion. It seemed that when the first settlers arrived, not long after the country was opened up by Burke and Wills, there had been some fairly bloody skirmishes between black and white. However, the younger Aborigines eventually drifted into the cattle stations, accepting work as stockmen or housemaids. They were soon followed by their relatives, parents, brothers, sisters, cousins and all, who generally camped a mile or two away from the homestead but were given (somewhat reluctantly at times) meat, flour, cloth and, when necessary, medical attention, by the station managers.

This worked out well for the stations, as they paid the Aboriginal workers very little compared to white workers—the savings being, of course, only partly depleted by the cost of killing an extra bullock or two to feed the tribe. The tribe, while it stayed, provided a cheap source of extra labour for busy times such as mustering. This led to a somewhat patronising attitude towards the Aborigines, but they, for their part, did obtain some benefit from such an arrangement: they were able to live together as a people and thus retain some of their tribal identity, some of their customs, and feel that even if they were not treated as equals they were needed and accepted, and to some extent cared for.

The money that the workers earned was used by all to provide the few luxuries obtainable in these parts (rum, blankets, a trip to town and so on), the necessities being provided by the station. But in 1965, apparently, the 'ignorant Southerners' stepped in and granted equal pay for Aborigines. It had been well meant, and done in a spirit of equality for all, but round here it spelled disaster for the very people it was intended to help. Employers still felt obliged to feed, clothe and care for relatives of

▲ Aboriginal stockmen like these now enjoy greater prosperity than in the last two decades, when many lost their jobs. Government grants have enabled some to buy their own cattle stations.

their Aboriginal employees, so it suddenly became cheaper for a station to take in a single young white man than to employ an Aborigine and become involved with his family.

The introduction of trail bikes and helicopters for mustering, requiring skills few Aborigines had acquired, worsened the situation for them. They went from being the backbone of the cattle industry to being unemployed; many drifted into shanty towns, and lived on child endowment and unemployment cheques.

'Couldn't the Aborigines be given back the land, or at least enough land for them to become self-sufficient?' I asked.

'Wouldn't do 'em much good now,' I was told.

The main tribal camps had been sited on the most reliable waterhole in each region. When the stations were established, or a township built, these prime

◀ This incongruous sight reflects the impact of technology on farming. With some cattle stations being many thousands of square miles in area, it is certainly a lot easier to muster by helicopter than on horseback!

sites were invariably commandeered; most other waterholes were not reliable enough to live on. In addition, overgrazing by cattle and scrub-cutting in drought years had altered the country to such an extent that it would now be very hard to live off the land in the traditional sense. Even if a group of Aborigines had the funds to set up a cattle venture on the land, the industry was in such a shaky state that it would probably fail.

The future, I was told, looked grim. This train of thought was interrupted by the arrival of the men's wives and children, happy and smiling after a party. Most of the men who had just been talking were married to Aboriginal women and their children generally had Aboriginal features, so their interest in the plight of these people was understandable. Happily, since my expedition this dreadful situation has eased, and many Aborigines have returned to working as stockmen—a profession to which they bring skills unmatched by any white man.

Chilbi returned soon afterwards, and we pulled our coats up around us before trudging back through the long grass to the far-off glow of the campfire. The others were already fast asleep and Paddy was snoring softly as we crept into our swags.

The Dreamtime

JAMES COOK described the Aborigines whom he encountered on his historic Australian voyage of 1768–70 as 'far more happier than we Europeans'. The key to their happiness, he saw, lay in the strength of their bonds with the land in which they lived—bonds that 'civilised' Europeans had long since broken.

For the Aborigines seen by Cook were not only dependent on the land for food, but also revered the land itself as sacred. In their eyes, their ancestors, who the Aborigines believed were part animal and part human, actually created the rocks, rivers and trees around them. When the ancestors died, they became incorporated into these features, and their spirits were still present in them. For example, one of the domes of the Olgas, a group of rounded rocks in Central Australia, is said to be the body of a kangaroo man who died, cradled in his sister's arms, after dingoes attacked him. The Aborigines call this time when their world was created (a time outside ordinary time) the Dreamtime.

The Dreamtime is a collective belief in which all Aborigines share, but each individual also has his own personal creation story, known as the Dreaming. According to this, every person is a direct descendant of a particular Dreamtime ancestor, whose spirit in turn becomes a totem for that person. In life, the connection between men and their totems is expressed through music, dance and art; in death, the human spirit returns to the rock or river or forest that is the home of its totemic Dreamtime spirit.

◀ **The influence of Christianity is in evidence at this otherwise traditional Melville Island burial site.**

▲ **This didgeridoo player's music, headdress and body paint all express bonds with his fellows and his totems.**

▲ Tribal members reach the climax of their kangaroo dance. Such dances reaffirm the relationship between men and their spiritual totems—in this case, kangaroos—so as to maintain harmony between them.

▲ The design this man is applying to his face is no random one. It follows a prescribed form he cannot change, and symbolises his tribe and his totem.

◀ Using diagrams in the sand, a mother teaches her children about their Dreaming—the story of how they are related to totemic spirits.

Sand paintings like this one, made using different coloured gravels, tell stories in their patterns about events that happened in the Dreamtime. ▶

CHAPTER 5

Into the Tropics

AWN AT BEDOURIE brought with it a gentle breeze which stirred the grass around us while we marched. We headed north, moving along the foot of a majestic dune which ran for mile after mile. The going was good: firm ground and a gentle breeze, with both the camels and ourselves picking up a good stride. The miles rolled past. Coasting along on Ginger, I had that marvellous sensation of being on a sailing boat, moving in a light breeze.

After lunch, though, things took a different turn: the breeze dropped and Cleo, who was in the number-two position, started to pull back, halting progress every few yards. Finally she was removed and tied on at the rear, Frances being promoted to number two. This improved matters only a little, and it was hard,

The soft, rounded forms of these large dunes are ever-changing, as the wind endlessly shifts the sand around. The rich ochre colour of so much of the sand in Australia is due to the presence in it of iron oxide. ▶

hot work, the going rougher now that we were on the western flat of the Eyre Creek flood plain. By 4.30pm we were dog-tired, and seeing tall timber not far to the east we made for it, to discover a fine pool of water at the foot of very high steep banks. We decided to camp early and checked out each of the camels.

Cleo appeared to have lost condition a little, and was stone-sore on the heel of her right forefoot. The pack sore on Frances had almost healed, but Walloper's sinew and muscle was now noticeable beneath his skin. Checking the stores we found that the sugar supply in our fortnight's ration kit was almost gone. We unpacked the radio and set the aerial up for a routine test. What with all the rolling round it took on the backs of camels, and being loaded on and off each day, we were always just that little bit relieved to hear 'Loud and clear' from a distant cattle station.

That night I treated the team to an old camp recipe. I shaved the biltong into fine pieces, removed the mouldy outside of the bacon and cut the partially mouldy inside into small cubes; these I boiled along with whatever dried fruit or vegetables came to hand, then added garlic salt and a few beef cubes. Meanwhile, I boiled rice in the other billy, drained it and tipped the meat broth over it.

My back, which had been playing up for a few days now, kept me awake for a little while before the cosy glow of the fire and the familiar movement of the

stars across the heavens lulled me to sleep. The problem dated back to the night I graduated as a veterinary surgeon, when my classmates and I held a celebration on a farm a few miles from Brisbane. As the evening drew on the party became somewhat unruly, culminating in a bareback bronco-riding contest by moonlight. At first my ride went wonderfully, but then I was thrown by a sudden swerve and landed on my rump, compressing a couple of discs in my back. The condition flared up from time to time, causing sudden and quite intense pain.

In the morning the pain had gone. As we prepared to break camp we were spotted by three Land-Rovers full of tourists (or 'terrorists', as Paddy called them). They came over and delayed us by asking interminable questions and, to add insult to injury, insisted on posing for photos with us and the camels. When we finally did get away, they beeped their horns in loud farewell, which sent the camels scattering. We had begun to find that civilisation, when we encountered it, was an intrusion into our private lives; it was as if *they* had turned into aliens, not ourselves.

From the time of that incident, Frances did not settle down. She would lag back until her lead-rope was strained, then break into a trot, forcing all behind her to follow suit. Worse, the number-two camel's lead-rope was tied to the back of the saddle on the number-one camel (Ginger), which Paddy and myself rode in turn. When Frances pulled back, the gentle rhythm of the ride was broken with a sharp tug which jarred the rider's whole body, and caused his bottom to hit the saddle hard and his knees to chafe against the iron mid-hoop of the saddle. Both men and camels were getting short-tempered in the heat, and the air that day was filled with language probably not heard there since the last bullock team passed through.

▲ Aboriginal boys play on a camel saddle, a metal frame with padded leather panels attached to it and, in this case, a comfy sheepskin seat.

The country was still much the same the next day, only now some stony ridges replaced the dunes to the west, but claypans still stretched to the eastern horizon. A movement up ahead under a stunted mulga bush caught Frankie's sharp eye, 'Marloo! Marloo!' They were far away and very alert, and when the Winchester kicked up dust some yards short, a big buck and two does bounded away to disappear across a stony scree to the north. Disappointed, we paused for lunch under the bush the roos had just vacated. We could still smell the musky scent of the big buck. The jolting ride of the morning had rubbed a hole in the seam of one of the water bags, so only half a cup of water was allowed per man, and each person's swig was watched carefully by the other three.

Before proceeding, we tied a nose-line to Frances. The mere knowledge that the peg was there did the trick—no longer did we have the lag-and-rush progress of the morning's march. We made good miles, even though the heat was intense and generated a series of incredible 'willy-willies'—small whirlwinds rising hundreds of feet in the super-heated air. There were numerous big clumps of dry

◀ A 'willy-willy' spirals up from an outback road. These vortices of hot air can reach heights of several hundred feet and travel along at up to 20 miles an hour.

saltbush here, and the willy-willies picked these up and whirled them around at tremendous speeds before they got too high and dropped to earth again. One passed within a few yards of us, but only the slightest breeze could be felt from it and the camels took no notice of it at all.

A large rocky mountain rose out of the plain bearing east by north, and provoked an argument between Paddy and me as to our exact location. It was finally marked as 'PD' (Position Doubtful) on our map, the only description we would both accept. Disputes between us were inevitable—such close and arduous companionship would have strained the patience of characters far saintlier than us.

A Touch of Empire

In midafternoon we crossed a flood plain two or three miles wide. Among some of the channels there was an odd, shallow mud pool surrounded by mud flats cracked by the heat like a shattered saucer, where birdlife clung on tenaciously: the tracks of emus were visible beside a few of the stagnant wallows, and pigeons, finches, wagtails and galahs rose noisily as we passed.

The map showed a homestead northwest of here, Breadalbane, where we hoped to buy a new water bag, and, if possible, some sugar. After half an hour the windmill came in sight, but the place was abandoned—or almost abandoned: two dingoes shot out of the fallen-down chicken run as we approached. The door hung on one hinge and a loose roofing sheet creaked as it swung to and fro in the hot wind. It had been well looked after once, a nice homestead, and someone had planted trees and shrubs to make a home of it. Most were now withered stumps, but one tree clung on and was in full blossom. As we headed off, dry and disappointed, we passed a solitary grave not far from the homestead,

▲ **This isolated grave expresses poignantly the loneliness of life—and death—in the outback.**

the paint blistered off the wooden headstone. Leaning at a slight angle, with the hot westerly whistling through the dead grass around it, the grave had an aura of incredible loneliness and desolation.

As we stood there a battered car came towards us along a bush track, leaving a trail of dust behind it, before clattering to a halt beside us. The driver was an elderly Englishwoman, a delightful character. It turned out she had spent the last few years driving around the Australian back country on her own; her equipment was spartan but functional. She asked us where the track led.

'Bedourie, about forty miles.'

'That will do nicely, thank you,' she replied.

As she had no sugar, which we could have done with, nor we any petrol, which she could have done with, we wished each other luck and went our separate ways. Paddy and I agreed that it was women like her who had made the British Empire what it once was!

We trudged on and the countryside took on a familiar appearance with stony ridges, heat haze and mirages. As the camels were now moving well we kept going in order to put this country behind us, hoping to find water up ahead in a creekline clearly marked on the map, Thogomora Creek.

At the end of nearly thirty miles we reached the creek at last light. It was a dry gully with a few sparse trees but no water. We unloaded the camels in the creekbed and after a lukewarm cup of soup each we fell asleep on our swags, my back troubling me again and reminding me of Burke and Wills—they too had suffered pains in back and legs, probably from all the riding. Dingoes howled to the west and south of us, perhaps the ones we had disturbed at Breadalbane. None of us really cared very much.

Dawn of August 17 was overcast, but the clouds cleared as the sun rose over the eastern plains. High stony ridges stood to the west, while we travelled largely over the flat country alongside the Georgina River. The ground was well covered with native clover and yellowcap, which gave the countryside a lush and attractive appearance. Unfortunately, it also concealed gilgais and large cracks in the dry soil into which we stumbled with monotonous regularity.

The Georgina River, in the dry season, hardly justified the term, and was a flat plain about fifteen miles wide, rutted with numerous small creeklines—all dry, except for the occasional perennial waterhole. In contrast Burke and Wills came through here in the wet season. Wills noted that Camp 87, almost exactly on the Tropic of Capricorn, was on a creek with two or three small waterholes, and that the previous night they had camped on 'a fine creek two chains [132 feet] wide and fifteen feet deep'.

Looking at the maps, it became evident that they were slowing down across this flood plain, managing only fifteen miles a day at the most. Perhaps the strain of the journey was already starting to tell, or perhaps they were simply giving the camels a bit of a break and feeding them up on the excellent browse.

For our part we were being very cautious of the browse on this plain, for a highly poisonous tree, *Acacia georginae* (or Georgina wattle) was supposed to grow here. It could cause rapid deaths in stock hungry enough to eat it. Sure enough, soon we found it in abundance, growing on nearly all the creeklines—a twisted, distorted-looking tree with drab olive leaves; even the seedpods were shrivelled and misshapen. To my horror, when I pointed it out to the others, Chilbi told me 'the camels bin eatin' 'em that fella las' night'. He had been unaware of its poisonous nature because Georgina wattle did not grow in his area of the country.

We kept on, crossing the Tropic of Capricorn with no sense of elation, just glancing anxiously at the camels from time to time. After a while we ceased to worry.

A Gift of Sugar

As if to stress the fact that the tropics started at the Tropic of Capricorn, the day became desperately hot—and of course the leaking water bag meant short rations for all. Paddy trudged on in the lead, head down and whistling determinedly. It's an ill wind, though, that brings no good: the short water ration caused him to miss every second note.

In his notes for this leg of the journey, Wills, after mentioning that they camped on the Tropic line, remarked that he had taken some good latitudes at his last camp. Latitude observations gave a traveller a good idea how far he was north or south of the Equator—or, in Wills's case, just how far he had to go to reach the Gulf. But Wills was, as far as I could see, not taking star sightings for longitude, which would have told him how far east or west he was. Longitudes required much more time and took fairly complex mathematics to compute.

▲ Gum trees line the banks of what has been and probably will again be a creek, but is now just a channel of dry sand.

They had largely relied on their compass to point them north and only paused to take latitudes, their sole interest now being how far they still had to go.

This meant that they would in fact have been heading about six degrees to the east of north: compasses here are out by that margin, and over 1,000 miles that error would have pushed them fifty miles or more off course. This, then, would explain why, although aiming for the Albert River, they arrived eventually at the Flinders River, a good way to the east. They had no way of knowing that the magnetic forces of this area would affect their compass.

All thirsty thoughts these, as for mile after mile we headed across numerous dry creekbeds. Ahead, on the other side of the flat, we could make out high downs country, and agreed that it would be good going—that anything would be good going after the undulations of the creekbeds. However, when we got up to them the downs proved to be covered with some of the worst stone we had yet encountered, great sharp rocks the size of footballs. We would have been better off staying on the creekbeds.

The late-afternoon sun picked out the roof of the Marion Downs homestead to the north, and we reached it, tired and thirsty, at sunset. The children of the homestead raced out to witness our strange cavalcade, and, in return for water and a jar of sugar, we gave them each a ride on a camel. The manager of the cattle station was away, and his wife was holding the fort, as wives have done since pioneering days. She was, as it turned out, an avid botanist, and was making a study of the local wild flowers; her hobby was reflected in the pretty flowerbeds and well-watered lawns. We left at twilight, waving goodbye to the children and promising to try to collect any unusual flowers for her. Alas, we never did.

We pitched camp beside a stagnant waterhole, and brewed many a billy to make tea in which to enjoy our newly acquired sugar. It may have been the children, or the homely atmosphere of the station, but something had touched a chord in me and I lay awake thinking of my family and home. None of Burke's party had had family to consider, so none was torn between looking back and looking ahead.

I lay listening to the familiar night sounds—the frogs and crickets, the chirping of a small bat overhead, the crackle of the fire, the clink of the camel bell and the wind in the trees above us. Paddy always slept the sleep of the just, and was able to finish his tea and be asleep before his cup was cold. Chilbi had a snore like an old cross-cut saw and he too slept soundly, for a campfire had for many years been all the home he needed. Frankie slept lightly, and occasionally had bad dreams, calling out in his own Aranda tongue before settling back to sleep. I understood his apprehensions and wondered what life had in store for this shy youth with the flashing grin, or, for that matter, what life would offer most of his people in the future. A dingo called far off as I gradually settled down, and I dreamt of children playing with building blocks in front of a fireplace.

Alternative Cuisine

Next morning, dreams over, we saw signs of wild pig everywhere as we loaded up the camels. Domestic animals that had reverted to the wild, these pigs were messy animals, fouling each waterhole they found and spreading such unsavoury diseases as tuberculosis and leptospirosis. But they had one saving grace: they were meat—always assuming that you were quick enough to kill one.

This black boar is a wild descendant of domestic pigs imported in the 18th and 19th centuries. Feral pigs quickly established themselves over large areas of northern and eastern Australia, where their propensity to carry diseases makes them a serious pest to humans and livestock alike. ▼

We saw our first pig only five miles out from camp, a big black boar grazing half a mile to the west. Paddy, the best shot among us, grabbed the rifle and ran bent double down a shallow gully, keeping out of sight of the big boar and circling to get downwind of him. After a couple of hundred yards the gully ran out and Paddy was forced to stalk the pig through open grassland, moving one slow step at a time, freezing whenever the boar looked up. We held our breaths in silence. I was trying to remember the smell of roast pork; Chilbi and Frankie, from a very different region, were staring at their first wild pig. The boar was aware that something was going on and his whole frame was tense and alert, snout sniffing the air and ears pricked. Paddy was just within firing range for the old Winchester, and was slowly raising the rifle to his shoulder.

Just then, tired of being made to stand still, Ginger let out his mighty groaning bellow and the boar took off. Paddy managed to hit it a glancing blow but the pig disappeared into a ravine thick with tangled lignum bush. As Paddy raced in after him we could hear other pigs moving excitedly down the ravine, but our breadwinner re-emerged, scratched, hot and empty-handed. With a surprisingly moderate curse for Ginger, he took the lead-rope and headed off again, moving across a soft loamy plain. In the distant timberline to the west we could make out a herd of pigs grazing happily, but we marched on with disdain, for we could spare no time for long hunts.

It dawned on me that this had probably been the main reason why Burke and Wills did not live off the land more. Any animals within a couple of hundred yards of a camel train were certainly aware of its presence and thus very hard to approach, and to leave the train and walk half a mile, stalk for fifteen minutes and then walk back empty-handed was a great time-waster— especially since the team took a fair while to fall back into rhythm.

On this day, however, we were in luck, for late that morning a red marloo doe broke cover from a thorn bush only fifty yards away, and Paddy dispatched her with one shot from the saddle. She was in excellent condition with no young in her pouch—a prize for any tucker-bag.

Chilbi prepared her quickly, removing both hind haunches and tail and scrapping

▲ Just part of the 6,000-mile-long fence that was erected to keep dingoes away from valuable livestock in New South Wales, Queensland and South Australia.

the rest. This was usually done, he told me, when the hunter was too far away to carry back the whole carcass, or when there were only a few mouths to feed. The haunch and tail represented only about half the weight of the carcass, but contained over eighty-five per cent of the meat on the roo, and almost all the body fat, so it seemed a sensible manoeuvre. Why carry double the weight back to get only the last fifteen-per-cent morsel of food?

Happily supplied with supper now, we moved on past a supposedly dingo-proof fence with dingo tracks on both sides and going right through it, and then near another fence we met a man in his utility vehicle trying valiantly to muster up some scrub cattle, only to send half of them bolting through the fence, and wrecking his gearbox in the process. There was a good camp near a waterhole up about ten miles, he said. We couldn't miss it—big tall trees all along it.

We pushed on again for another ten miles, but found no tall timber. By now the light was fading, so we made for a group of saplings where Frankie had seen corellas heading at drinking time. As we topped a gentle rise above this muddy soak, another herd of startled pigs scattered squealing in all directions, one of them falling to beady-eyed Paddy and the faithful Winchester.

None of the others knew how to butcher a pig, or to check it for the various worms and diseases pigs carry, so the task was left to me. While Frankie got the fire going, Chilbi came over to view my handiwork. He asked me why I opened up the belly and I explained that it was to check for disease. To illustrate, I pointed out the kidneys, which I had discarded since they were full of worms, and tried to explain about checking a beast's organs for signs of tuberculosis, but his interest waned.

I realised that our two systems of meat harvesting once again represented the evolution of two different cultures. Our forefathers in the northern hemisphere harvested cattle and pigs—both carriers of tuberculosis and other potential dangers for man. The meat often had to be stored for a long time, so it was bled out and meticulously guarded against the build-up of bacteria. Chilbi's system, on the other hand, evolved where meat could never be stored anyway, where tuberculosis did not exist, and where the main danger lay in attracting flies by opening up the abdomen.

Unfortunately, there was not enough water to wash the blood from my hands and arms, and while the pigmeat smelled delicious cooking in the coals, it did not taste so good with the smell of warm blood all over me, and the million or so flies that were attracted to it.

In the last rays of the sun, the corellas—which had been wheeling and screeching in droves over-head—finally settled down, to have their place in the sky taken by thousands of small bats. Later, an enormous feral cat came snooping round the carcass of the pig, his eyes glowing like coals in the firelight.

I lay back on my swag enjoying the sensation of my belly being full of meat, pondering the fact that Chilbi would not eat pork while Frankie happily gulped one piece after another, in between bits of roo. Chilbi obviously made no connection between this new food source and our salted bacon which he happily ate, and regarded this white man's 'delicacy', pig, with much the same enthusiasm as a member of the Melbourne Club would view goanna, a large lizard much favoured by the Aborigines.

Feral cats have established themselves in every part of Australia since early colonial days. In the wild natural selection has produced specimens that can be twice the size of their domestic ancestors. ▼

We got away early next morning, and had covered three miles before we came to the waterhole we had been told about. This was a pretty consistent finding on our trip: people in the age of motorised transport had lost all sense of distance. After all, a hole ten miles away took them twenty minutes to reach by car, and one thirteen miles away took only six minutes extra. But by camel, that extra hour's three-mile walk could mean the difference between reaching the water before sunset or not. After a while it became a game to ask a person how far off such-and-such a place was, and then see how far it actually was. Most people could not tell within ten miles how far they had driven that day. Stockmen or drovers, however, were generally correct to within half an inch or so of the nearest waterhole.

Boulia

The country started to change dramatically. We were now passing through thick black-wattle scrub, some of which was in full golden blossom, and here for the first time we saw the mistletoe bird fluttering from one wattle spray to another. This beautiful bird is the size of a finch, his plumage a gleaming blue–black with a bright scarlet chest and sickle-shaped beak. The creekbeds and river flats were marked by huge ghost gums rather than coolabah, and kingfishers and rainbow birds flew between them as we passed.

Fences were becoming more and more numerous, indicating a closely settled region, and we tried to save time by following a road to our next

▲ **Kangaroo meat roasts gently on an Aboriginal campfire. The four sand goannas in the foreground will make a delicious second course.**

stop, the little township of Boulia. We were forced off the road seven times in two hours by gigantic road trains, each consisting of a semitrailer with an extra two trailers in tow. Their dust, and the fact that we had to get off the road and halt while they went past, made for miserable progress.

We paused about 11am to share the last of our water, about a mouthful each, and headed off again munching on a piece of pork and a piece of roo each. Boulia was only a few hours' march away, and there we were to have a rest day.

We hoped for mail in the town, and the probability of good grazing on the banks of its permanent waterhole suggested that it would be an excellent campsite.

It is amazing how interminable and tiring those last few miles before a rest can be, but by midafternoon we had finally arrived on the south bank of the Burke River, at what was regarded by local tradition as having been Burke's campsite on January 8 or 9, 1861.

Across the river, and only a few hundred yards away, stood Boulia, Paddy's mecca, for he had it on good authority from drovers that they sold chocolate there. After the camels were unloaded and hobbled, the gear stowed and swags unrolled, we set out for the town. Sure enough, it had a café which offered not only chocolate but also milkshakes and proper 'tailor-mades' (commercially manufactured cigarettes).

We collected the small amount of mail that had made its way through a mail strike, and repaired to camp for an afternoon nap. Paddy swallowed the last of his chocolate in a gulp, pulled his hat over his eyes and was asleep. I took my boots off and turned to my mail.

The first item was a postcard from an aunt in Copenhagen, with a picture of the Little Mermaid. I felt she would have looked even more tranquil beside the waterhole here. The second item was a letter from a friend who had trekked alone through remote areas of southwest Tasmania on foot. He bid me good going, and remarked '…the first part of any journey is the simplest, relying only on physical strength. The next few hundred miles need determination.' How right he was. In lighter vein, he had included the centrefold of the previous month's *Playboy* magazine to keep us company over the mountains.

A massive three-sectioned road train powers its way across the outback, sending up clouds of dust from the dirt road. ▼

In reply, I sent a radio-telegram, coded so as not to offend delicate ears which might be listening on the air:

'Grateful for US survey map stop general outlines appear extremely favourable stop however details vague stop please send latest edition stop if that not possible send us original ore bodies for analysis stop. NOVEMBER GOLF OSCAR.'

I heard later that my friend (who had evidently forgotten about the contents of his original letter) spent a long time pondering that telegram before he deciphered it.

That night we wended our way up to the hotel in Boulia for a few quiet beers and were soon asked to a party by a group of local Aborigines. Paddy and Frankie decided to turn in early—after a hard day Paddy liked nothing better than his bed, and Frankie was shy with strangers—but Chilbi and I set off in the dark trying to follow the vague directions we had been given. On the way, we

The small town of Boulia receives much of its water supply from this primitive riverside pump. ▶

were talking about the stars and navigation, and I asked Chilbi about his people, and how they used to navigate. He said they never used the stars. Instead, he said simply, 'They look all around them.'

I thought I knew what he meant. When I was a boy I knew that if I rode over to the big hill with one tree, followed the river down until it passed through some blackberry bushes and turned towards the three boulders, I would find a deep pond with fish in it. Was it like that, just knowing the country and keeping an eye on which way and how far you had come? A bit like that, Chilbi agreed, and there were always tracks, signs, marks. I nodded, thinking to myself that his idea of tracks and marks was like our idea of stars: they were there to help you if you knew which ones to look for.

When I came to think about this later the obvious sense of it came to me. Even with a modern sextant and computer, I could not pinpoint my position to within a square mile. Back in the Stony Desert, had we missed the soak at Bloodwood by fifty yards we could have perished. So, for a limited area— say a tribal territory in the desert—our system was useless; theirs was functional. Ours, of course, excelled where vast distances were involved, especially where there were no landmarks and the target was large—say a sea voyage where one is heading for an island ten miles wide.

The talk of navigation closed as we came into a clearing where the Boulia Aborigines were holding their moonlit party beneath a big kurrajong tree. Beer and wine had replaced the pitchery of Burke and Wills's time, but the hospitality was exactly the same, and Chilbi was treated with a great deal of respect and courtesy because of his age and bearing. The party went on well into the night before the singing started, but the old tunes had gone, replaced with modern country-style favourites by Slim Dusty, and such classics as 'The Pub With No Beer'.

Death of a Dog

The next day passed rapidly, a rest day with each man attending to his chores. Paddy sweated profusely as he tried soldering up one of the water tanks which was leaking worse than before.

We set out the following morning across a grassy plain, running parallel with the Burke River, determined to get the miles behind us before the day got too hot.

The water tank which Paddy had tried to repair was if anything leaking rather more and was almost totally useless.

Not long after Paddy took over the lead walk from me, a pick-up truck overtook us. The driver was Bob—owner of the café at Boulia—asking if I could come back to town to treat his bitch, which had been run over. I hushed Cleo down and quickly unhooked the medical bag, but it was to be of little use because, just when we needed it, everything inside it was in a dreadful mess. Bottles of disinfectants, anaesthetics, antibiotics and antiemetics were shattered, tubes of antihistamines and tropical lotions had been squashed, and bottles of tablets had popped open. In consequence the inside of the bag was coated with a foul medicinal glue which could cure any known disease if only someone knew how to use it. I located a few surgical instruments and wiped them, salvaged some camel anaesthetic and headed back to town.

The bitch was in shock and one hind leg was shattered beyond repair; it had to be amputated. A table in the café was scrubbed clean, and Sister Wendy from the hospital helped with some human anaesthetic and suture material, but I had barely begun the operation before I realised that we simply did not have good enough facilities. As well as the leg injury the bitch turned out to have a shattered pelvis, with no chance of repairing that on a café table. I asked for a rifle to destroy the poor beast, and was given a light Russian rifle which I fired at her skull point-blank. The gun was only powerful enough to penetrate the skin and awaken the bitch from her anaesthetised state into one of bewildered agony. Five shots it took—an experience I hope never to repeat as long as I live.

Bob, meanwhile, had left us to it and had occupied himself looking for something to replace our leaky water tank. He managed to locate two old cameleers' water drums on a nearby station. They had probably lain there for fifty years, but still held water. While we were testing the tanks our old photographer friend Joe Scherschel from the *National Geographic* turned up and offered to drive me out to the team, so we headed off and caught up with them about fifteen miles out. I thanked Joe for the ride and, somewhat subdued, took hold of the lead-rope. No one asked how the operation had gone. They were all pretty hot and tired, especially Paddy who as leader had done all the walking, and it was probably obvious from my manner that things had not gone well. We pushed on, hoping to make the Five Mile Lagoon by nightfall, but darkness overtook us, so we camped on a claypan instead.

Frankie had shot a kangaroo while I was in town, so we prepared our evening meal. The inner thigh muscles were taken first and grilled in the coals; the stronger and more sinewy muscles were cut into slabs and thrown in the billy with salt and dried onions; and Chilbi did his speciality of the chef, the tail. It was thrown in the fire—skin, fur and all—and left there until the hair was fairly well singed. It was then pulled out to cool off, at which point it was scraped with a knife to remove the remaining singed hairs. Then a shallow trench was dug and filled with warm coals, the tail placed in it, and covered with more coals. Too hot and it burnt; too cool, it was ghastly and greasy. But cooked just so, as Chilbi did it, it was a delight, tasting like a rather gamy oxtail. For the connoisseur, the skin should be removed before eating, and on a poor specimen the last six inches of tail are not worth bothering with, but dogs love it.

Not far from us were camped a couple of journalists who had driven down from Mount Isa to interview us. We spoke to them briefly, but we found their presence intrusive. What is more we did not (sour grapes) want to smell their sweet-and-sour pork cooking, and they most certainly did not want to smell our marloo, so we stayed in separate camps. We could see their fire through the trees: an immense blaze in comparison with our meagre 'black-man's fire'.

Any bushman worth his salt can tell the difference between the remains of a white-man's and a black-man's fire by the fact that the latter is composed of a small pile of well-burned sticks, the former by several half-burned logs. Most whites will explain this by saying that the Aborigines are too lazy to collect any more than they have to, but most white campers have no need to conserve wood. Tribes of fifteen to fifty Aborigines need a number of fires each night: they some-times camp on the one waterhole for three or four months, and if they were to light white-man's fires they would clear out all the useful wood for miles around. (It is interesting that a white person will happily burn two weeks' supply of wood in one night's camping, but at home turns the stove off as soon as a meal is cooked so as not to waste gas.)

Another reason for small campfires was pointed out to me once by a doctor working on an Aboriginal mission. Since the fires were, by necessity, open fires and the centre of the social group, there was a tremendous incidence of body burns in children under two years of age who had toddled or crawled into the fire. A white-man's fire would constitute an enormously greater risk of more serious burns.

▲ The Aboriginal equivalent of a barbecue: two kangaroos (lying head to head) cook slowly in a pit filled with coals.

The thought of burns reminded me suddenly that I had one last piece of roo cooking in the coals; it was difficult to distinguish from the other coals until we broke it open and knocked the burnt outside off. Frankie and I had half each, then turned in.

I had a dreadful night, trying to devise humane ways of putting down a dog that wouldn't die. Restless and half asleep, I heard the clink of camel hobbles beside me and for some reason imagined that Larrikin, like the dog, had returned from the dead to reproach me. I sat bolt upright, only to find gentle Cleo standing a yard or so away chewing the cud, silhouetted against the moon-light. Reassured, I lay back again, comfortable on the soft clay, and slept soundly.

The Last of Channel Country

Dawn of August 22 saw us on the march across a flat Mitchell-grass plain inter-spersed with low patches of scrub. By now slow and steady had paid off and we were catching up with Burke and Wills, whose progress had been reduced to a plod.

Roo and emu were plentiful but very, very wary, seen only as fleeting objects in the distance. Occasionally, if one seemed to be moving a little more slowly, or had pulled up to hide behind a patch of myall or black wattle, one of us would head off, crouched in a run, to try to close on it. We had no success at all; once aware of the presence of the camels the game was on hair-trigger alert, and we were so low on ammunition we could not waste any on long-distance shots or moving targets.

There were probably fewer (but more naive) targets on this plain when Burke and Wills passed, for the limiting factor in red kangaroo populations is permanent water, of which in those days before windmills there was less. The red kangaroo is a large animal—adult males can stand seven foot tall when on tiptoe—and they must drink water every four days or so during summer in these parts. This means they can only venture two days or so away from a permanent waterhole. In drought years that two-day radius is soon eaten out, and the population crashes if the drought is prolonged; at first the does simply fail to conceive, then the joeys in the pouch die, and later the adults too start dying.

When the white man came here he certainly caused hardship for the red kangaroo with his guns and dogs, as well as with his rabbits, cattle and horses eating their food, but all this was more than offset by the wells and boreholes he sank, providing permanent water. Oddly, this same change had a detrimental effect on the Aborigines, who had relied heavily on the wildlife congregating

The Dingo's Dominion

FEW SENSATIONS CAN BE AS EERIE for the outback adventurer as the creeping awareness that comes over one, while lying beside glowing campfire embers in the gathering dark, of being watched. Sure enough, next morning telltale animal tracks around the camp betray the presence of a hungry dingo, on the lookout for scraps of food.

In Australia one is never very far from a dingo, as the species' range extends over the whole continent. They seem archetypically Australian, but probably came from Southeast Asia 4–5,000 years ago, either with seafaring traders or with a late wave of Aboriginal settlers. Dingoes remained faithful friends of the Aborigines, who apparently used them as hunting dogs or just pets. (They reportedly made excellent bedwarmers on cold winter nights!)

To many Australians, though, the dingo constitutes a pest. Its taste for

▲ A family of dingoes plays in a moonlit glade. These wild dogs can be tamed as pets.

sheep has led to the construction of the longest fence in the world—longer than the Great Wall of China at over 6,000 miles—running through South Australia and Queensland.

Dingoes also threaten the survival of other animals by competing for the same prey. Such competition led to the

extinction on the mainland about 2,000 years ago of a marsupial wild dog called the striped thylacine. The thylacine then became confined to Tasmania—where the dingo has never become established—and it is thought to still exist today (although sightings are unconfirmed).

around waterholes in dry years but now found that the animals had dispersed to bores too brackish for man to drink and therefore out of bounds.

There are a lot of well-meant words spoken about the 'endangered' red kangaroo, but they only distract attention from the animals really needing protection: the little numbats, bettongs and bandicoots. All these small marsupials live on the insects and plant roots of the bushland floor and have suffered terribly as their territory has been cleared and burned for pasture.

We plodded across many small, dry creekbeds on the plain, all of which in this region were lined with Noogoora burr, a noxious weed. The burr was especially annoying to us as it worked its way inside socks and trousers, and, even worse, under saddles, where it wore sores very quickly. In addition to the Noogoora burr, the creeks we crossed had another poisonous plant growing along their banks—*Acacia georginae* again, this time in great abundance. These plants are seldom eaten by livestock but they are unwelcome because they invade prime growing sites once inhabited by more palatable species.

▲ A prettily marked numbat forages for termites with its fast-flicking tongue. Once widespread in Australia, numbats are now in dramatic decline, and this is probably due to a combination of land clearance, bushfires, drought and predation.

As for the camels, Frances's pack sore was not healing as well as we had hoped. What she really needed was a rest from carrying a pack, a spell long enough to enable scar tissue to form. Still, she kept up the pace and had not lost much condition compared to some of the others.

Up ahead I noticed the sails of a bore about a mile to the east of our path.

'Hey Paddy, water ahead! Time to fill our tanks, old buddy.'

'Ahead? You mean half a day's walk sideways, mate. There'll be more further on.'

'No sign of it.'

'Trust me.'

For once I trusted him and we lunched beside a waterhole on Wills Creek, which the original expedition had crossed on January 10, 1861. The flies were very bad, coating our boiled kangaroo meat in a seething opalescent mass, which Paddy christened 'roo garni'. In fact he had a colourful saying for just about every aspect of our humdrum lives. While others might go to the waterhole 'for a drink of water', Paddy would go to 'rinse his guts out'.

We were to rinse our guts out properly that night, for late in the afternoon we passed the homestead of the large Two Rivers cattle station, the home of Jack and Josephine Clarence, who invited us to dinner. We pushed on for another hour before setting camp on a creekbed, then left the camels and returned to the homestead on foot in our none-too-splendid best gear. Our hosts treated us with typical country hospitality, and the food and drink were a vast improvement on tea and roo garni.

Tired and well fed we trooped back to our camp—which took an hour to find, as the dying embers of the campfire were hidden by the high creek banks. It was a memorable farewell to the Channel Country.

▲ *Acacia georginae* **may look an attractive shrub, but it is in fact poisonous and can lead to the death of animals that eat it. This strategy helps ensure the plant's survival.**

▲ **Crocodiles only have to open their mouths for one to understand why they have no natural predators other than man, and he only dares approach if armed with an unnatural advantage—a gun!**

Attack and Defence: The Keys to Survival

STAYING ALIVE is the ultimate challenge for every living thing on earth, and Australian animals and plants are no exception, displaying a wide range of survival strategies.

One life-preserving approach that is particularly useful to plants is unpalatability. *Acacia georginae*, for instance, contains potentially deadly poisons which deter grazing animals. Animals can be unpalatable too: the spiked cones all over the body of the Moloch or thorny devil lizard would make even the hungriest predator think twice about this meal! Another lizard with a cunning survival ploy is the frilled lizard, which frightens off predators by raising a huge ruff of skin around its neck, making itself look several times its real size. Many lizards also use camouflage as defence, but the supreme example of this in Australia is surely the tawny frogmouth. This strange-looking bird is nocturnal, so it needs to be secure when it sleeps during the day. Its plumage so perfectly matches the mottled bark of its tree-roost that any predator would be hard pressed to spot it.

They say, however, that the best form of defence is attack—a principle employed to painful effect by the bulldog ant, which inflicts a poisonous sting on any intruders. For two of Australia's most feared creatures, defence and attack are performed using the same weapons. The venom of the deadly fierce snake is injected indiscriminately into its prey or into a menacing intruder. Just the fear of this lethal weapon is enough to deter most attackers, and the same is true of that other supreme killer, the crocodile; whether attacking or defending, the resulting carnage is the same.

◀ **The fierce snake, which can grow to eight feet long, is the most venomous land snake in the world. Such a weapon provides simultaneously for superb defence and attack.**

▲ The thorny devil lizard's impenetrable-looking armour deters predators, but the thorns also guide dewdrops into channels on the lizard's skin and from there into its mouth.

◄ An alarmed frilled lizard has fled to the safety of a termite mound, from where it is trying to scare off its aggressor—in this case a harmless photographer—with its huge frill.

▲ Bulldog ants have huge mandibles for biting their predators and long tails for stinging them. These formidable ants only occur in Australia. They can grow over an inch long, and can jump as far as seven or eight inches.

◄ A pair of tawny frogmouths streamline themselves against a branch, their eyes closed, maximising the effect of their camouflage. They will remain motionless in this position until danger has passed.

CHAPTER 6

Land of the Kalkadoons

OUR ROUTE NORTH TOOK US PAST WINDSOR PARK, a beautiful cattle station but so alien to its English namesake that whoever named it must have been drunk or blindly nostalgic. The breeze blew from the southwest, moving the Mitchell grass gently around us and keeping the flies away. It was a beautiful day, the sky cloudless and the air crystal-clear. A vast rolling plain stretched ahead of us, with blue mountain ranges looming far off to the north and west.

As we marched across the plain I noticed that my shadow no longer had a belly on it, and on closer inspection neither did I. So absorbed was I in examining

▲ A peregrine falcon on the lookout for prey soars sideways through the air. When the prey is spotted, the bird will dive at 200 miles an hour, making it the fastest of all hawks.

my newly visible ribs that I almost trod on a grass snake, one of many we saw that morning. The tracks of others were everywhere on the plain and they were obviously faring well on the abundant quail, lizards and native mice. A pair of falcons circled overhead, keeping an eye open for small animals disturbed by our passage.

We had finally faced the truth that morning that our pork was no longer slightly off: it was rancid, and we jettisoned the putrid green slabs to lighten the loads. We halted for lunch on a slope, stone ranges now clearly visible ahead. The breeze had dropped, and the sun burned down on the open plain as we squatted down to finish the last of the roo garni. It tasted just a tiny bit off, but we had worked up an appetite so it was still '*kurra marra*' (good meat) to us. The brief meal over, we stood up, brushed the dust off, stuck our hats back on, and turned to face the ranges. We weren't too worried by them because we had met an old roo shooter just south of Windsor Park who had told us there was a track through them. Roo shooters are solitary souls—a breed apart, eking out an existence shooting kangaroos for their skins, which are sought after by the fine leather industry. They tend to have a pretty basic view of life; you would not care for your daughter to marry one.

There may have been a track through the Swift Hills in his time, but he was over eighty; there was no sign of one now, and it was the cruellest ground I have ever dragged an animal over. The ranges were broken sharp sandstone rising to a ridge every half mile, then dropping abruptly into a gully again. The camels strained up the loose shingle on the climbs and slipped and slid down the other side. Every so often we had to cross limestone outcrops, some as smooth as a marble floor, others broken into sharp piles of rubble. This was also our first taste of

◀ Gum tree and desert
flowers cling precariously
to life atop a rubble-
strewn outcrop of rock.

mountain spinifex, a large bushy grass with long spiky leaves which penetrated trousers and skin, leaving our legs covered in itchy sores. Our faces and arms were suffering as well, striped in welts from the thick acacia scrub which branched exactly at the height of a traveller's eye. It seemed that it would never end, mile after mile of climbing, falling, spinifex, limestone, acacia and flies.

Exhausted, we stopped and called a half-hour break to rest the camels. It has been said that the whole mass of ranges which now lay before us was once a gigantic island, some 20,000 square miles in extent, set in an ancient freshwater sea. Thus the limestone on which we now stood was part of a fossilised coral reef. A few yards away from us lay an unusual formation of stone. It was the entrance to an enormous cave, the mouth of which was about fifteen feet across. The cave itself went straight down into the range—a vertical drop of at least sixty feet, as near as we could judge by the sound of falling stones. The entrance lay in such a position that it would catch a lot of the run-off from the ridge; thus the cave had probably been carved out by water. But where did the water go then? We reckoned that that cave must either go for miles and empty out on the plain, or else contain within it an enormous reservoir which gradually seeped away.

Nearby an echidna's tracks meandered off to the right. Echidnas are small primitive mammals that resemble nothing so much as a miniature porcupine. As I followed the tracks wondering idly what echidnas tasted like, I noticed three stone spires across a valley to the east, lit up by the afternoon sun. These were the three cones Wills had described! As they made their weary way back from the Gulf, he had written:

▲ Though you would never guess from its appearance, the echidna, or spiny anteater, is a relative of the duck-billed platypus. Both are monotremes, an ancient order of mammals that has only one other member, the long-beaked echidna which is found in New Guinea.

'Wednesday, March 20, 1861. Camp 32R…We started at a quarter to six, but were continually pulled up by billabongs and branch creeks, and soon had to camp for the night. At the junction of the two creeks just above are the three cones, which are three remarkable small hills to the eastward.'

This was a tremendous find, as a number of historians have believed that the return journey was made a hundred or so miles east of here. Yet there the cones stood, a geomorphological feature so unique that there could no longer be any doubt as to the return route. While blazes on trees can be forged or obliterated, three rocks cannot; they stand as eternal monuments.

Back on Track

And it was to be within another hour that we made our second discovery. Having toiled over more of the broken sandstone ridges, we looked north and saw that we were almost over them; but we saw more than that.

On Saturday, January 12, 1861, Wills wrote in his diary:

'We then entered a series of slaty, low, sandstone ranges…The more stony portions are, however, covered in porcupine grass, and here and there with mallee…We had a pretty good view of the country towards the north. As far as we could see in the distance, and bearing due north, was a large range…The east end of this range just comes to magnetic north. On the west of this, and bearing NNW [north–northwest], is a single conical peak, the top of which only is visible…From here a descent of two miles brought us to a creek…'

And there it all was, laid out before us just as Wills had described it: 'The Brothers' and 'O'Hara's Gap' to the north, appearing as a solid range, and

'The Monument', a solitary sandstone spike bearing nearly north by northwest. (As has already been pointed out, Wills was not aware of compass error in this region, so his compass bearings were about six degrees out.) Below us, about two miles off, was the creek on which he and Burke had camped.

My calculations showed, to my delight, that they had passed only a couple of hundred yards to the west of where we now stood. By working back from this point, using Wills's diary and the few cryptic comments left by Burke and King, we could, as a result of today's discoveries, reconstruct their progress throughout this region both going up and returning. Until now this had been a matter of academic guesswork.

Our elation was dampened by the fact that both Paddy and I had, for the last few hours, been suffering from the most dreadful stomach cramps and diarrhoea, which were probably the result of elderly roo garni. We made for the creek below as quickly as our exhausted camels could travel, unpacked and searched through the ruins of the medical kit for a suitable cure, which thank God we found intact. Reduced now to biltong and dried peas for the main course, we ate greedily. To celebrate the day's discoveries I opened one of our six tins of peaches in syrup, and we divided these between us like four hungry dogs, despite the stomach cramps.

Paddy, a seasoned cameleer, is pictured here on a previous expedition in the outback. ▼

Wills remarked of their camp on this creek that 'we found here numerous indications of blacks having been here, but saw nothing of them'. They may have seen nothing of the Aborigines, but the latter were following their progress very carefully. King reports that 'when we came in sight of ranges ahead we saw several volumes of smoke to the east and west'. These were not wisps from tiny cooking fires: they were the signal fires of the Kalkadoons. Without being aware of it, Burke and Wills had just entered the territory of a mountain tribe of Aborigines, who were later to resist the takeover of their land in a series of bloody encounters with white prospectors and settlers. The progress of the first white men ever to come here was in fact followed closely both on their way north and on their return.

One prospector, S.E. Pearson, who was looking for copper in these mountains twenty-odd years after the event, ran across quite a number of elderly Kalkadoons who had been eyewitnesses to the passing of Burke's expedition through their country. They told him that, as the explorers were making their way south through the ranges on their return journey, some of the young bloods of the tribe had decided to attack them. To prepare themselves the warriors feasted on kangaroo meat and doubtless painted war stripes on their chests with the bright ochres for which the region was famous.

Kalkadoon Conflict

WHEN THE EXPLORERS Burke and Wills, in 1861, first made their way through the rocky landscape that lies between the Georgina and Corella rivers in western Queensland, they were unaware that they were trespassing on the territory of the Kalkadoon (or Kalkatungu) tribe of Aborigines. Where Burke and Wills had gone, a steady trickle of farmers and hopeful prospectors soon followed. The Kalkadoons initially welcomed the newcomers, often acting as guides and labourers. But when gold and other minerals were discovered in the area in the 1870s, outsiders began to flood in. Competition for land created tensions between the settlers and the Kalkadoons, erupting into violence in 1878.

The Kalkadoons began using guerrilla-style tactics to try to oust the invaders, springing surprise attacks on them and then disappearing back into the hills. But when, in 1883, the Kalkadoons massacred five mounted policemen brought in to quell the disturbances,

▲ As Europeans pushed further into the outback, expropriating Aboriginal land, conflicts often flared up like that recorded here by Thomas Baines (1822–75).

matters came to a head. The authorities sent in heavily armed troops, and in 1884 a pitched battle took place at Prospector Creek. The spears of the Kalkadoons proved no match for the white men's guns, and their resistance was crushed, bringing the tribe's death toll for the six years of conflict to 900, and finally establishing the loss of their lands.

It is unlikely that the members of Burke's party were in any state to withstand an ambush, but their camels were to save them. There are three things camels detest above all else—mountains, mud and hard work—and as the expedition made its way south through the ranges in pouring rain the combination of all three would have upset them considerably. Now when a camel is upset (as I know only too well) it lets out a roar like a constipated dragon. Even when one is used to camels it is a frightful noise, and the Kalkadoons were so terrified by these unfamiliar animals that they called off the ambush. For once Allah was on Burke's side.

Bickering

The course next day was determined for us, as it had been for Burke and Wills. Ranges closed in to the west and east, and there was a wide grassy plain to the north, so we packed up the camels, uttered our early-morning 'Let's hit the road again' war cry, at which the camels would lurch to their feet in their back-and-forward manner, and headed due north. The camels moved very slowly that day. The bumping and bruising by packsaddles as we crossed the range had aggravated old pack sores and started new ones. Flies which were attracted to the weeping sores for moisture caused them to become infected, and a camel's woolly fleece is an ideal habitat for maggots to grow. We were in trouble, for in the winter months the unpleasant skin disease known as fly-strike was the last problem I had expected, and with our limited medical kit we were almost powerless to deal with it. The problem vexed me as we trudged north.

Up ahead, about half a mile off our path, the sails of a bore were visible, so I suggested that we pull up and fill the water tanks there. Paddy argued that the mile there and back was not worth it, and that we would get water later in the day. It was hardly a new situation, and we bickered for a mile or more on the matter. Finally we agreed that if there were cattle there, and thus water, we would cross and fill up. This time I was right: there were cattle, so we filled up.

On any trek like this personal differences show up, magnified by the isolation. Paddy and I were very different people but both fairly determined, so we argued over the minor things that were made to seem so important in our long, dreary day's march. On occasions we seemed subconsciously to seek arguments simply to give our minds something to do.

'How far to Pilgrim Way?'

'About sixteen miles.'

'I make it nearer seventeen.'

(Pause while map and ruler come out.)

'Sixteen point four miles.'

'Was nearer seventeen when I asked.'

'Bull!'

Our basic approach to problems was different as well. I have always preferred to sit back and weigh up all the factors I could think of before deciding anything, thus at times missing opportunities when they arose. In contrast, Paddy seemed to me to leap in and do things without bothering to consider the risks, so at times we each made errors that riled the other. But such different approaches were also essential in our team, for we faced many problems that required them. While I might spend half an hour prodding and poking at a camel before I eventually figured out what his bellowing was about, it was Paddy who first had to fight the cranky brute to a standstill, throw him, and then hold him down while I did my prodding and poking.

I reflected as I walked along that a similar relationship must have developed on the original expedition. Wills was a meticulous scientist and well organised, but he lacked colour and flair; he was not a leader. Burke, on the other hand, was hopelessly ignorant of rationing, or navigation, or organising his men, but he had the dash and charisma of a natural leader; men either loathed him and left him, or followed him—even to their deaths. Between them they held qualities that are rare today. We ourselves certainly could not pretend to have them; perhaps our era does not produce the sort of man to whom success is more important than life itself.

The imposing Selwyn Ranges looked no less daunting to the author than they did to Burke and Wills on their pioneering expedition. ▶

His party must have been a little apprehensive, though, as they marched across this plain towards Pilgrim Creek, for the grim nature of the Selwyn Ranges was clearly visible from here—ironstone skeletons of a Precambrian range crumbling into jagged ridges. To the west the Standish Ranges, while blurred by distance, were even more menacing, growing higher and merging with the Selwyns on the northern horizon. The Kalkadoons, watching silently from their mountains, must have thought the expedition ludicrously tiny and frail as it wandered across the plain, heading due north to the mountain passes.

The plain consisted of rolling Mitchell-grass flats crossed by a number of dry creekbeds lined with spinifex. The flats were broken up by occasional patches of mallee scrub and low rocky outcrops. The creeks had colourful names which left the traveller wondering about their origins. Prickly Bush Creek was obviously well named, and Dead Horse Gully was self-explanatory, too, but what of Monastery Creek, where there was of course no monastery at all? What story, for that matter, lay behind the name of Petticoat Creek? All these creeks were dry, and they would not contain water until the wet season, in summer; even then they would merit the name 'creek' for only a few days at any one stretch.

Unsurprisingly, we winter travellers struck no more water that day until sundown when we trudged up to Pilgrim Well, a bore at the junction of Petticoat, Pilgrim and Yellow Waterhole creeks, and probably the site of Burke's Camp 93:

▲ The evening aerobatics of pink and grey galahs are one of the great spectacles of the outback.

> 'Situate[d] at the junction of three sandy creeks in which there is an abundance of water. The sand is loose and the water permeates freely, so that the latter may be obtained delightfully cool and clear by sinking anywhere in the bed of the creeks.'

This might have been so back in 1861 when Burke was camped here, but over a century later we found that the creek water tasted strongly of cow dung; even the bore water from Pilgrim Well, which we might have expected to be high in revolting magnesium and calcium salts, tasted better. The birds thought so too: thousands of galahs descended to drink at nightfall while cattle wandered over to our campfire and gazed at us as we chewed our tough biltong. We were meat-hungry again and the thought of fresh steak was quite appealing, but it was not done to shoot and eat someone else's bullock without asking first. We tried

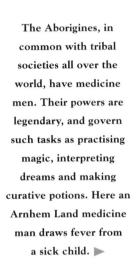

The Aborigines, in common with tribal societies all over the world, have medicine men. Their powers are legendary, and govern such tasks as practising magic, interpreting dreams and making curative potions. Here an Arnhem Land medicine man draws fever from a sick child. ▶

to sing them to death with a ceremonial curse, as we thought Aboriginal medicine men might have done, calling them into the cooking pot. No law against that. 'Here, bullock-bullock. Die, bullock-bullock.' No response. No steak. Back to biltong.

Camel Alert

We had now covered 645 miles from the Dig Tree in the last thirty-four days, but we were still a day behind Burke, and still had 300 miles yet to go.

Two options were open for that day's journey. We could travel due north from here and cross a saddle on the eastern end of Mount Collis, or we could go further east and cross the rise near O'Hara's Gap. From where we were the latter appeared easier going, and after the rough ranges two days earlier even Burke would probably have chosen this course.

The country ahead was thick mulga for some miles, and then opened out onto Mitchell-grass downs. The mulga slowed down our progress a little, but once on the downs the camels strode out, and we had covered a mile or more before Chilbi's sharp eyes picked out something. We were travelling with six camels, so that Chilbi, on Alice at the rear of the column, had been watching the tracks of five camels. But now he saw six sets. Checking the tracks of all of ours, we realised that we had crossed the tracks of an enormous wild bull camel. The tracks were fresh: two cigarettes old, Chilbi reckoned—in our terms about half an hour.

Once or twice each year bull camels come into season, or 'musth', like elephants, a condition in which they become extremely aggressive. Such a beast had recently attacked four motorists in Saudi Arabia, killing three and nearly scalping the fourth. By his tracks, this one—which was at least as big as Walloper—was moving about quite rapidly. We had only one bullet left for the Winchester. We now carried it loaded for the first time on the trip, and we pushed on warily, spotting freshly browsed desert oak here and there which marked his progress. Judging by the height of the oaks he was a very big camel. Thank God we never met him.

Around morning break we came across another set of tracks—a female camel and a newborn baby; the mother's tracks were of similar size and spacing to Alice's, while the baby's tracks were tiny by comparison and took three steps to her one, not always in the same direction. We thought for a while of going after her, as breeding camels and calves both fetch good prices nowadays. But we had to push on, and our camels by now were looking so poor it was doubtful if we could have run her down in any case.

By lunchtime we had headed out into fairly open country, and we started seeing marloo—first one, then a few, then hundreds. As luck would have it our last bullet was wasted on the first one we saw. After that we saw them in droves, either moving off slowly as we approached or lying quietly on their sides beneath scrawny acacia bush, quietly passing the heat of day.

The thermometer showed over 100°F by lunchtime and for the first time the presence of moisture was noticeable in the air—it no longer had the ability to dry sweat instantly the way it did back in the Stony Desert. The air was still and heavy as we hushed down near O'Hara's Gap for lunch— a treasured piece of salami each, some dates and a couple of figs, which were covered in ants and tasted like formic acid. The salami was going off a bit too, but the dates were pleasant enough.

Lunch over, we faced a broad sweeping slope covered in three-foot-high grass. It was scarred at irregular intervals with deep erosion gullies which had us detouring more than progressing. The long grass made a swishing noise as we filed through, and numerous small grass snakes slithered out of our way. They are quite harmless, but where they occurred in large numbers like this you generally found that living off them were the larger taipans and brown snakes—not so harmless. I wished the long grass would not make that swishing noise.

In any event we descended the slope unscathed and after two miles entered thick scrub. The afternoon sun baked down on us as we pushed on, plagued by black bush flies attracted by the sweat on our faces and the sores on Cleo, who had been off-loaded.

It was still hot and sticky by mid-afternoon when we encountered three men from a rig team at Boomerang Bore. They were pumping the water tank full as the windmill that would normally do the job was useless without wind. 'Twelve miles to Devoncourt,' we were told. A moment of self-congratulation for Paddy

▲ The venom of the eastern brown snake contains a potent toxin that acts immediately on the central nervous system of its victims, causing paralysis and rapid death.

and me, as we had both calculated our distance covered that day to the nearest hundred yards and were both right on target.

The sandy soil over which we now travelled was marked more and more frequently with camel tracks. The acacia and casuarina scrub lining the winding creekbeds had obviously been browsed in the last few weeks, but the camels that had browsed them managed to stay out of sight. At last, just on dusk, we limped down onto Sandy Creek, a tributary of the Cloncurry River, and followed it until we hit a cool shallow pool shaded by tall trees.

The camels, once unsaddled, headed down to the creek to slurp up a couple of dozen gallons each before shuffling off to graze as fast as their hobbles would allow them. Cleo's hip showed white in the gathering darkness where the white paste coated her pack sore. The night fell swiftly and became suddenly quite cold. We rolled out our swags and lay back around the fire watching the billy boil and the biltong stew bubble away. For a change we were to have rice with it.

Our old friend Joe Scherschel, the photographer from *National Geographic*, drove down from a homestead a few miles away (we had been in touch with him over the flying-doctor radio) and offered to drive us to the pub for a beer before we turned in. We obliged him like a shot. It was a strange sensation to be in a car covering thirty miles an hour or more, and I noticed that we all tended to hang on tightly.

The pub was a small, weatherboard structure with a wide verandah badly in need of repair. A couple of old-timers propped up the far end of the bar; otherwise it was deserted. The barman lifted his head off the bar and eyed us suspiciously. 'What do you bloody want?' was his hospitable greeting. 'Beer,' we said, and he peered at us for a while as though we had replied in Urdu, then shuffled off slowly to find some beer.

Our appearance *was* a bit off-putting: bluey coats pulled up around our ears, hair now long and matted, and our faces streaked with the sweat and dust of the last few hundred miles. Come to think of it, our smell was probably a bit off, too.

Eventually we were each handed a warm bottle of beer and the bottle-opener was pointed out to us; then the barman turned his back while he counted the change, coin by coin. It was an enjoyable night apart from that, for a few more locals drifted in and we were soon sitting round yarning. A miner pushed his tin hat back and sang an aria in Italian as we left.

Home in camp once more we stoked the campfire and put the billy on for a late night cuppa. We had done 126 miles in the last five days, the camels were tiring, and Walloper was stone-sore, so we reluctantly decided to camp here for a day. It would lose us twenty-four hours on Burke, but in the long run pushing on with a lame camel would have delayed us more.

Viceregal Visitation

We were rudely awoken as the dawn rang out with the sound of a herd of steers galloping past us to the waterhole. We had obviously camped too close to their drinking trail, and they must have been mustering up the courage to pass us all night, too stupid to find another path.

Still tired, I stretched, scratched my head a bit and looked around for the camels, then realised it was a rest day and settled back into the swag for an extra hour's kip. As I pushed my way into the swag the smell of fetid socks and feet emerged from its depths, but I dozed off anyway. Some time later I opened an eye and surveyed the scene. Chilbi had the fire going, its smoke drifting up through the river gums; Frankie was ambling back from the creek with a billy for tea; and Paddy had his socks off and was prying his toes apart. Between us we had devised a technique to determine whether or not socks needed washing: you peeled them off and then flung them against a ghost gum; if they dropped off they were OK, but if they stuck to the tree you were due to wash them.

From Wills's diary it appears that the original team had few changes of clothing, and had probably felt just as grubby as we did. They would have understood our panic, therefore, when we heard that the Queensland State Governor and his wife had arrived at Devoncourt station from Brisbane and were being driven over to meet us. None of our usual rest-day routine today! The camp swung into frantic activity—mess gear washed in the creek, best shirts on, swags rolled, cake of germicidal soap dredged up from the bottom of the veterinary bag (and actually used), socks pulled off the ghost gums.

I cannot honestly say that we presented a splendid sight when the viceregal cavalcade appeared, but it was the best we had looked for some time, and we had dragged up sufficient logs for a traditional white-man's fire. As they shook hands with us I could distinctly smell their soap and I winced, hoping they could smell ours.

I need not have worried, for the visit was very friendly, and the people from Devoncourt had brought some glasses and cold drinks so we didn't have to take turns drinking tea out of our four chipped and stained enamel mugs as we had feared. In fact it was a relaxing afternoon, as the Governor was an ex-Navy navigator and quite interested in the navigational details we were investigating. He even offered some worthwhile bits of advice.

There was no need to stoke the fire after they had gone: it was still four or five times our usual size.

We were joined by our friend Joe and two other journalists, John and Bob, for tea that night. These two had been looking for us for a couple of days and finally contacted us during our test transmission. As they were twenty miles off course we had radioed them in. In gratitude John, a trained cook, made a very passable roo bourguignon with a roo Paddy had taken on a bullet they lent him. Just then, Paddy's sister and brother-in-law drove up too and joined our camp for the night. Radio reports of our progress were attracting a lot of public interest, and hearing that we were out of bullets and clean clothes (we only had two changes of outfit to start with), they had followed the reporters out with a load of supplies.

The clean clothes, the day's rest, the company and the bonfire all combined to give our camp a festive feeling, and we sat around the fire yarning long after the moon was up. Over a cuppa we found out what was happening in the outside world. There had been a postal strike, and Parramatta were odds-on for the football premiership. Many people had phoned the radio stations—some to say they were interested in our trip, others to offer copious advice, and a few cranks to say we were just a bunch of ratbags.

And where, I was asked, were we going from here? I had to admit I was baffled. We had definitely been on Burke and Wills's track, or within half a mile of it, back at the Swift Hills, but from Pilgrim Well there were no entries in Wills's diary for five days. King mentioned in his undated notes that after the slaty ranges they had passed over well-grassed, well-watered country for sixty miles until they came to a dead stop, 'nothing to be seen but ranges'. That would be about here somewhere. They had then apparently tried to cut through the ranges to the west but had failed and returned east. Wills's next entry, on January 19, 1861, had them crossing the range at about this latitude, but no one knew exactly where. Burke, in one of his brief notes, remarked the next day that he determined to go 'straight at the ranges'.

It left us with many choices, but the option of following Burke straight through the ranges, with our camels as tired as they were, did not seem a realistic one. What is more, when there was an easy way out, and other factors were equal, I could be as weak as the next man, so I chose to go north–northwest and then turn through the mountains via the well-worn Chinaman's Creek Pass. As we busied ourselves breaking camp at dawn we shared a sense of apprehension, however, for it was still not going to be any picnic.

We Lose the Track

We led the camels down along the riverbed as the sun rose over the craggy peaks of the Selwyns, striking the upper branches of the white gums above us. It was such a beautiful morning—crisp and cool, with soft powdery soil underfoot—that Paddy and I walked along together leading the camels and singing in rough-and-ready harmonies that I fear did not greatly enhance the beauty of the morning; looking back, I saw Chilbi grimacing theatrically and covering his ears. He and his son did sing occasionally, but the sound was more a murmur than a song—soft and undulating like a running brook or the drone of honeybees.

After a few miles winding through the riverine mallee flats, we passed the Devoncourt homestead and said farewell to our hosts and our visitors of yesterday. Already the heat of the sun could be felt, and once off the river flats the ground started to become harder and more stony. The rises at first were almost imperceptible—nothing more than flinty downs country such as we had met before—but gradually the inclines became steeper, the gibbers larger, and Walloper became more and more difficult to manage. The ranges around us were dotted with gnarled and stunted acacia bushes with the odd grass tree starting to appear.

These grass trees had a ten-foot sooty black trunk crowned with a tussock of grass-like leaves, from which protruded a huge six-foot spike. These made excellent spear shafts, according to Chilbi, but I knew that if the leaves were eaten by cattle they caused a peculiar brain-cell degeneration. In some areas the disease was called 'wamp', reproducing the sound the affected livestock made when they finally toppled over. They did not get up again. So here was yet another plant which I hoped our omnivorous camels would pass over.

We had come fifteen miles by lunchtime and as we crossed the next creek we saw a delightful waterhole to which we made our way, two blue cranes taking off as we approached. The banks of this creek, like so many others, were lined with Noogoora burr but we managed to find a clear patch of earth beneath a river gum. Opposite us a tiny kingfisher perched on a dead branch, eyeing the fish below him, the smallest of which was twice his size. His lunch, if he caught one, would be substantially better than ours.

We hit the road as soon as our meal was swallowed and soon found ourselves climbing a steep ridge and entering a narrow pass between high mountains. By now Walloper was nigh-on unmanageable, pulling back every ten paces. And when Walloper pulled back the lead camel was brought to a jarring halt and the others shuffled along to a standstill. His feet had been stone-sore ever since we

▲ **These huge flower spikes are just the upper part of grass trees. Below the grassy leaves lie another 10 feet of solid trunk. The trees can live for several hundred years.**

crossed the Swift Hills; the gibber here was loose and tumbled under his big pads, bruising them further. We made it over the ridge and halted for a while to rest him, flopping down ourselves while we were at it.

The narrow pass through which we had just come widened here into a valley about half a mile across. The waterway continued down its length, meandering along through open woodland; slender trees grew on the sketchy clay-and-shingle plain, which was marked everywhere by termite mounds—brick red in colour and about two feet high. They gave the upper reaches of the valley the appearance of a rusty graveyard. Between them were scattered tussocks of spinifex and dry spear-grass.

The valley was surrounded by the remains of a once majestic range. The crumbling cores still stood like old mountain fortresses perched on the rubble slopes of their former grandeur, eroding in the heat and wind.

The architecture of the wild has many marvels, but one of the most remarkable is the termite mound. These living rocks, made using soil, chewed wood and faeces, contain chambers in which the termites live and work. ▶

'Which way do you reckon that Burke fellow went, Chilbi?' I asked.

He considered. 'This way, I reckon. Follow creekbed.'

'Why this way? This creek runs into hills. Maybe Burke thought it finish up there.'

'No, this river go straight through all right.' He took me over to the bank and pointed out the signs. 'See up there in trees. Grass and sticks from big floods all bent one way. Water move that way plenty fast. River not stop at mountains, go through all way.'

The signs of a path through the mountains were clear enough, for those with eyes to see. But did Burke have such eyes? It seemed unlikely. I had entertained a vague hope that this creek, Chinaman's Creek, was the actual one down which Burke had come, but the further we advanced along it the less it fitted Wills's description since the alignment was wrong.

Lower down the valley its appearance improved a little: the black trunks of ironbarks (a species of eucalyptus with roundish, blue–grey leaves) stood out among golden strands of wattle, and the course of the creek was marked by white ghost gums. A tall shrub was in flower, large purple blooms growing off its spindly tangled stems, but these odd splashes of colour seemed out of place in this inhospitable part of the world.

It was late in the afternoon, when the valley was in shadow and the sun lit up the peaks to the east, that we were hit by locusts. At first the odd one, then a few more at decreasing intervals, then literally thousand upon thousand of them smacked

▲ Ironbarks, conspicuous with their dark, furrowed bark, are one of over 500 different species of eucalyptus tree.

into us, disturbed from feeding on the bushes as we passed. Overhead they swirled in a silvery-grey cloud which lasted for miles. We reached the end of it only shortly before camp.

The ground here was still stony—a poor campsite with little suitable camel feed and no water—but the camels had had enough work for one day. Walloper had been a little better in the afternoon but not much, and both Cleo and Frances were tiring badly. That night I could not get comfortable, wriggle and dig as much as I might. Each gibber I took away merely made the ground more uneven. Even Paddy slept badly, cursing Walloper and Frances in his dreams. The camels stayed nearby, too knocked up to scout out the sparse vegetation available.

Family Festival

We were up stiff and sore before Orion faded in the dawn, and we saddled and left the spot without breakfast, without talking, without even a glance back. To us it was not a site worth remembering, which was unfortunate as we left our camel bell there somewhere.

The valley was still in deep misty shadow but the cliffs and spires above us were bathed in sunlight and the first heat of the day reflected down from them. The creek disappeared through a narrow cleft in the cliffs which I had originally hoped to be the gap mentioned by Wills—a spot he described as 'the most dangerous part of our journey'. But although man had altered the narrow pass since Burke's day by pushing a railway and a road through, there was enough relatively undisturbed ground to see that this stretch would have been in no way as dangerous as some of the country they had crossed earlier. Certainly the cliffs rose high and sheer on each side and were pocked by fissures and caves, but the watercourse itself would have offered reasonable going for them.

Chinaman's Creek, then, was not what Wills had described as the 'upper reaches of the Cloncurry', along which they had travelled. It was, however, on the edge of Kalkadoon lands, so we searched for any of the crane's-foot paintings on rock faces which the Kalkadoons used to mark out their boundary. We saw none. Disappointed, we pressed on, heading northeast up a wide valley, and again encountered the locusts in their millions. There was scant vegetation here to attract them, but what little there was they were demolishing at an incredible rate.

Although isolated low ranges still stood ahead to the west and northeast, the countryside now took on a much gentler appearance—more rolling slopes with soil covering their rocky frames. Fence lines started to appear more frequently and soon after midday we struck the bitumen road which ran from Cloncurry to the town of Mount Isa. Some miles to the west of us the Cloncurry Shire Council had erected a stone cairn on this road with an inscription stating that Burke and Wills had passed through there on January 22, 1861. If this was accurate then they would indeed have been heading for the Corella River and not the Upper Cloncurry.

The heat was such that we had ceased to care much either way, but we forced ourselves and the camels to push on, to get this sticky, hot bitumen behind us. Cars hurtled past and honked their horns or pulled up in a screech of brakes and a cloud of dust, neither of which was welcomed. Alongside the road the white man had marked his domain with broken bottles, rusty cans and old newspapers, all presided over by billboards and messages exhorting passers-by to Keep Australia Beautiful.

Cleo had shown signs of fatigue early on in the day, and had started to sweat profusely. We off-loaded her onto Ginger and Paddy, and I had to walk all day. Generally speaking, when one day was the same as the next, without a definite goal beyond a good day's march, the timeless atmosphere of the bush pervaded everything and there was no rush. But this march on bitumen was dragging, and we were impatient to reach Cloncurry for an even more important reason: here we were to rest up for a few days with our families, who were flying up to meet us. It was galling to see the cars fly by or stop to tell us we were only nine or ten miles out—three hours' hard march for us but only ten minutes for them.

At long last we trudged into town from the west and crossed the Cloncurry River. A fair number of townspeople had come out to greet us, and the Shire

The expedition's progress was hampered by a swarm of locusts like this. This swarm is actually quite small: larger ones can cover an area of 400 square miles and include 50 thousand million locusts. ▼

Council had kindly made arrangements for the camels to be kept on a recreation ground while we were there.

We pulled up beside the first shop we saw and went in for a cold lemonade and, of course, some chocolate for Paddy. We were about to sit and enjoy ourselves when we heard a commotion outside, where our camels knelt resting on the roadside surrounded by goggle-eyed children. A very drunken stockman had decided to have a ride on Ginger, who was bellowing his disapproval and looked just about ready to bolt, straight through the surrounding children. Following a brief but heated discussion on the stupidity of taking a ride on someone else's camel, we headed off through town for the reserve, where we wearily began to unload. At that moment my wife and parents drove up, and all thoughts of Burke and Wills vanished in the happiness of our reunion, cries of 'I hardly recognised you, you're so thin' and 'God, you're filthy' offsetting the more affectionate remarks.

That night was like a fairytale, sitting round in a modern motel sipping champagne, smelling of soap and feeling the crisp sensation of a clean and ironed shirt. When I was combing my hair it had taken me time to reaccustom myself to the image in the mirror, my hand moving in what appeared to be the wrong way. Also the bed that night, though soft and clean, was just too yielding and insecure for sleep, which came only when I rolled my swag out on the wooden floor.

The next few days passed pleasantly, but, as always, there were a thousand-odd chores to be done.

Cleo's pack sore was worse despite antibiotic treatment and had formed an abscess which had to be lanced and drained. The four of us had a task to get her down and hold her there for treatment. Walloper's stone-sore feet were still tender, so we decided to try on a set of camel shoes. We had been told how to do this by an old camel hand: four ellipses were cut out of bullock-hide, each one large enough to fold up over the foot and draw loosely together with a rawhide thong at the fetlock. The whole process was nowhere near as easy as it sounded, particularly the part where you actually fitted the shoe onto the camel's foot. The recreation ground was quickly hidden beneath a swirling cloud of dust from which ropes, men or bucking camels emerged only momentarily. At last Walloper stood there, booted and quite disgusted, before taking his first tentative steps—high, obstacle-clearing steps. Within a short time, however, he was walking normally and we hoped the problem was solved. (Wills remarked at one stage that they had 'delayed for the purpose of getting the camels' shoes on—a matter in which we were eminently unsuccessful'.)

We also at last obtained some fly repellent for the pack sores from Mount Isa. Cash had to be wired through from down south, travelling stock permits were required, supplies had to be reorganised, and perished items discarded. But we had the easy jobs—or so we were told later, for my mother and my wife had offered to do our washing, seriously underestimating the task they were taking on.

In the local library and museum I spent absorbing hours poring over Lands Department maps of western Queensland on which each of Burke's camps had been marked in. The author of these unpublished maps was one Harry Towner,

The Central Hotel at Cloncurry, bathed in evening sunlight, advertises three of the things hot, weary outback travellers must long for: food, ice and beer!

a local who, like myself, had been merely an amateur historian but who had spent a lot of time searching through local records to locate marked trees thought to be on the explorer's track.

He showed the group well to the west of Cloncurry, and going north along the Corella and not the Cloncurry River; this proposition seemed as feasible as some of those shown on other historical maps in existence. In some areas Towner was obviously quite accurate—where, for example, he had shown them returning past the region of the three cones. In other spots, though, he seemed to have them much too far west, showing them almost due south of The Monument when Wills recorded that it bore north–northwest on the compass. Still, he had put in a lot of hard work, and had produced what was the most accurate map to date. I felt a bond of friendship and admiration for this man, whom I would sadly never meet since he had died some years back, his work unrecognised.

There was time for more than research. At lunch, over a cold draught beer, a quick glance down the menu showed no dates or damper, no roo garni. Good! The choice was either grilled local barramundi or rump steak. The barramundi, or 'barra', is a river fish that moves out to sea to spawn. In the south it is nearly always frozen and the sweetness destroyed, but here it was fresh, and in that state was probably the most beautiful eating fish on earth.

It was a strange sensation to have the family there. I had changed physically and mentally as the trip had progressed, and at first they seemed like strangers. But this sensation quickly wore off, and in what seemed no time at all they had to fly off while we still had so much to say to each other. As their little plane rose up over the ranges to the south and grew smaller, a tiny bright speck lost in the shimmering heat haze, we returned to the reserve and those chores which had, until now, been put aside for more convivial pastimes. It was time to get under way again.

Windmills like these are a common sight in the outback. They pump water up from deep beneath the ground, enabling people and animals to survive.

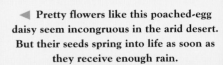

Baobabs have a natural insurance policy against drought: their colossal, bottle-shaped trunks are packed with water-retaining wood. In some cases, the trunks can reach a diameter of 60 feet.

Pretty flowers like this poached-egg daisy seem incongruous in the arid desert. But their seeds spring into life as soon as they receive enough rain.

Water in the 'Dead Heart' of Australia

EARLY EUROPEAN EXPLORERS in Australia, hoping to find great lakes or even an inland sea in the interior, were stunned to find an endless desert land of sand, rock and stones. According to a popular phrase of the time, the continent had a 'dead heart'. This is, however, far from true. It is a heart that has been the death of many, but it is not dead itself. Vast areas receive less than 10 inches of rain a year, but nevertheless many plants and animals do survive, with the help of special adaptations.

One of the creatures one least associates with desert habitats is the frog, yet Australia is home to frogs that can live outside water. Water-holding frogs absorb vast quantities of water through their skin when rain falls, which then sustains them while they hibernate underground until the next rains. Some plants work on the same principle, storing water in their leaves and stems. In the case of the baobab, or bottle tree, water is stored in tissues held in the great bulbous, bottle-like trunk, enabling it to survive long after the rains have gone. Other plants lack the ability to outlive drought in the way the bottle tree does. Instead, their seeds lie dormant beneath the sand—often for many years—until sufficient rain falls to allow them to germinate, flower and seed again. This phenomenon allows for one of the most spectacular sights the desert can offer, when, after rainfall, thousands of brilliant blooms suddenly daub the drab sands.

It is remarkable, given the very particular devices these desert-dwellers have evolved, that Man, who has no such built-in devices, is able to survive at all in such conditions. Yet survive he does, thanks to his ingenuity. Bores drilled deep in the desert bring precious underground water to the surface, enabling people to live, and even graze their livestock, in one of the most inhospitable regions on earth.

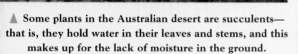

▲ Some plants in the Australian desert are succulents—that is, they hold water in their leaves and stems, and this makes up for the lack of moisture in the ground.

A thirsty Aboriginal stockman takes a reviving drink from a spring. He was lucky to find one with drinkable water, as many such natural springs are brackish. ▶

◀ This water-holding frog is enjoying the cool night air. Soon it will burrow underground, waiting there until the next rains—which could be as long as three years.

CHAPTER 7

The Plains of Promise

▲ Camels can get to 'bush tucker' way out of the reach of others.

NEXT DAY WE WERE UNDER WAY EARLY. As we crossed a broad plain back to the Cloncurry River I remembered that today was my wife's birthday, which we had in fact celebrated two days early, with champagne, in another world. Here, in the harsh world of reality, spinifex and anthills were looming up ahead. The terrain generally was characterised by the presence of peppermint gums, whose sky-blue leaves gave off a strong pepperminty smell when crushed.

Initially the countryside was marked by rough, stony hillocks which appeared to be rich in iron or some other metal, but later the country became flat, well timbered and generally covered in grass, and the first thorny acacias appeared. These are hardy shrubs growing to nine feet or so, their succulent leaves well out of reach of stock and protected by long vicious thorns pointing up towards the tip of the branches. To our camels, however, they were the right height for browsing, and the thorns were no problem. They searched out the base of a branch, grasped it between tongue and palate and pulled the branch down, stripping off the leaves and leaving the thorns still on the stem.

We paused for lunch beneath a tree on the dry bed of the Cloncurry River, the luxuries of town not quite forgotten as we returned without enthusiasm to our simple provisions. The riverbed was broad and sandy and scattered with flat stones of the sort little boys skip across smooth water. The massive river gums on the banks carried flood litter high in their branches—a reminder that the river was not always as we saw it.

After lunch we entered a thick eucalyptus woodland. As we made our way through the trees, parallel to the river, we saw the blue-winged kookaburra for the first time, perched high on an ironbark preening his beautiful plumage. Unlike the kookaburras in the south, this species, although noisy, never laughs—or, as one bushman put it, 'they only laugh when it snows in the Gulf'.

We camped not far from the river, and when we were unsaddling we noticed that Ginger was in pain from a nasty rash on an area where the padding had come away from his saddle and the exposed metal had rubbed. We treated him with Pharaoh's Brew and left him to wander off to join the others.

As we sat around the campfire we faced a dilemma—whether to follow the Cloncurry River, as most historians suggested Burke had done, or to cut north to the Corella River, as suggested by Towner. The description Wills gave of the river along which they had travelled matched our day's impression of the Cloncurry, but it seemed worthwhile to take a look at the Corella, too.

In the six weeks since we had left the Dig Tree we had covered 778 miles and were still not level with Burke's progress. Furthermore, 200 miles still remained between us and the shores of Carpentaria, and yet our allowed twelve weeks were already half gone. My ideas about the reasons for Burke's failure were not coming out right. Even if we were able to maintain this pace, our rations on the return trip would theoretically be very thin, as Burke's had been.

▲ Unlike the kookaburras in the south, the blue-winged kookaburra doesn't laugh, but it does use a high-pitched howling song at dawn and dusk to warn other birds to keep away from its territory.

Dawn saw us already on the march, the countryside similar to that of the previous day. There were a few wary kangaroos on the flats, and an occasional wallaby, and here and there some fairly old bustard tracks. We had been talking around the campfire the previous night about crocodiles, trying to explain to Chilbi and Frankie just what a crocodile was. As crocs are found only in the far north they are unknown to the peoples of the central desert. 'Big uncle of *perentie*' was as close as I could get. 'He lives all the time in big *kwaja*.' (By this I meant: a large animal related to the goanna and living in big waterholes.)

'How big this crocodile?' asked Frankie.

'Big as Walloper and Larrikin together,' I said, exaggerating somewhat, and watched his eyes enlarge and whiten in the firelight, darting all around us searching the darkness for this monster. Poor Frankie must have dreamt of crocs that night for he was up and off after the camels long before the sun was up.

For some time now Frankie and Chilbi had been taking on more tasks of their own volition. Between us we had overcome a hurdle in our relationship. What I had initially regarded as laziness on their part was in fact reluctance to show initiative for fear of offending. Many Aborigines have grown up with the knowledge that if a white man wants something done he bawls out an order, so that until that happens it is best to sit quietly and wait. For his part, the white man looks at the black man sitting there and concludes that he is just plain lazy. The trip would have been worth it if for no other reason than to find out that this barrier could be overcome by working together.

Without pausing for breakfast we set out north for the Corella River, marching along in the relatively cool morning air. We passed in turn through gidgee (a small acacia) scrub, ghost-gum woodland and grassy plains—the type of country which, in 1841, the explorer John Stokes had called 'The Plains of Promise'. The day grew warm once the sun was up, and by midday we were practically walking through a steam bath.

Walloper's new shoes were obviously causing him great discomfort, so we had to unload him and throw him down on his side to examine his feet. Not only had the shoes chafed the skin badly across the tops of his feet, but stones had also found their way inside to bruise the pads. Paddy flung the shoes away in disgust, muttering under his breath as we resumed the march.

The painted roof of the Clonagh cattle station hove into sight on the horizon, waving up and down in the oppressive haze. We pulled into the station to refill our water tanks. A horse in a nearby yard took one look at us and went berserk, racing round the yard and almost breaking through a post-and-rail fence in terror. A dozen or so other horses, though, took not the slightest notice. The incident appeared not to worry the manager, Nick Murray, or his wife, who treated us all to a sizable lunch. Unused to this ample fare during the day, both Paddy and I developed acute stomach pains as we rode that afternoon. We had to walk and walk until the pain finally eased. Finally at sunset we halted, throwing our swags down and falling upon them without further ado.

The End in Sight

Next morning we faced the Gulf Country, a crescent of black-soil plains 200 miles wide and stretching 400-odd miles around the Gulf of Carpentaria. The shores of the Gulf are lined with thick mangrove swamps, while the plain is interrupted in places by low ranges and is scarred by deep riverbeds. The rivers only run in the 'wet', carrying the run-off from the tropical downpours northwards to empty out into the shallow Gulf.

The wet can start any time from November onwards and continue through to March, turning the plains into an almost impassable quagmire. Only essential land maintenance is carried out during the wet, and those who stay on to do these chores have plenty of time on their hands to sweat, drink and sit listening to the rain. But in the cooler months, when the plains dry out and harden, the tempo of life quickens in time with the bellowing of the muster and the rumble of the road trains.

While the people of the Channel Country seemed as stoic and enduring as the dunes themselves, the men of the Gulf Country did everything at a break-neck pace, as if the wet might start tomorrow. They were a mixed and colourful lot: cattlemen and fishermen, prospectors and prawners, horse-breakers and croc-hunters, not to mention a strange human flotsam which had chosen to hide in this lost corner.

Some people had achieved legendary status: there was the hermit who lived in an old rainwater tank, and another who carefully tended a lawn bordered with bleached croc skulls. On one prawn trawler was a deckhand who had once, under another name, been a distinguished gynaecologist, while the skipper of another trawler could down a bottle of Scotch whisky without effect

◀ A Gulf Country man
and his dog take a break
from crab fishing.

but was moved to tears by a melody from his native Greece. The animals here were just as strange an assortment: crocodiles and deadly poisonous snakes, graceful brolgas and rare gold-shouldered parrots, agile wallabies and loose-skinned Brahman cattle.

When we reached the Corella River we found that it fitted Wills's description just as well as the Cloncurry, but we would now have to follow the Corella until the two rivers met together in a few days. By midmorning we were bashing our way through a thick, thorny-acacia scrub when, out in the western sky in broad daylight, we saw a bright meteor. This seemed to worry Chilbi deeply, for he asked me many questions about it.

Descending the high steep bank of the Corella, we followed along the riverbed for a time, but eventually decided it would be easier going and more direct back up on the plain. Getting up there again proved to be easier said than done, and the camels made hard work of the climb. But at last we made it, and all sat down to get our breath back.

On the bank to our left we saw our first palm tree, which coincided with the latitude given for Burke's Palm Tree Camp. This wasn't necessarily an indication of being on Burke's route, though, as these trees also occurred at about the same latitude on the Cloncurry. Away from the river bank the thorny acacia grew thicker than ever, and we set camp early, having reached a bore towards the northern edge of the scrub.

As we came into the clearing around the bore we surprised a herd of wild pigs coming in to water, and Paddy shot two. By the time the first stars came out we had pork legs roasting over a good fire, our only worries being Walloper's feet, which were still causing him trouble, and Cleo, whose pack abscess was not responding to treatment at all well.

The moon had barely risen when I got up and wandered the fifty yards or so through the acacia scrub to the bore. As I was bending down to fill up the billy, I heard a sound which made me freeze. Somewhere in the darkness behind me something was moving, slowly and quietly, towards me. In panic I swung at it with the only thing I had—a billy filled with water. The billy hit it and bounced off, clattering against the metal trough of the bore with a tremendous din. The creature gave a shrill squeal and bounded off. Several others answered with similar cries and disappeared into the thorny scrub. Pigs! I laughed a nervous, relieved laugh as people do in such circumstances, refilled the billy and returned to the campfire to tell my story. Chilbi and his son roared with laughter at my fears; it was a story which would be told and embellished around many campfires at my expense.

▲ Feral pigs wallow in a cooling waterhole. Such substantial animals provided welcome meals to the team.

Bushfire

Next morning, shortly after the start of the day's march, the river line broke up into numerous smaller channels and our path was frequently cut by small creeks, terrain in which it was impossible for camels to get into stride. Consulting the map we decided to head away from the river towards a windmill, which should soon have been visible on the horizon; from there we would follow a compass bearing of thirty-one degrees, which should put us back on the river just west of its junction with the Cloncurry. That was the plan.

We turned in the direction of the windmill and made our way across the plain, mile after mile of waist-high grass, a hot wind blowing in our faces. Perhaps it was the grass rustling in the wind or some other unknown cause, but the camels became jumpy and suddenly bolted, galloping across the plain, ropes parting as each camel went its separate way. We finally reassembled them and retrieved bits and pieces that had come adrift. Hot and sweaty, we shared a swig from the water bottle and a curse on the mysterious nature of camels, then headed off again.

The windmill loomed up considerably to the right of where we had calculated but, thinking little of this, we headed for it, reaching it about midday. The ground for half a mile around it was chopped up by the sharp hooves of cattle and boggy with urine and dung. The area was well populated with flies too, so we moved off half a mile before squatting in a dry gully for lunch.

A fence line stood nearby and I took a bearing along it, only to find nothing corresponding to it on the map. This started us rechecking and we found that we had taken three hours to reach a windmill that the map showed to be only about four miles east of where we had begun the day's march. Then it dawned on us that this was a new mill and that the mill shown on the map was gone. We argued back and forth as we finished our dried dates (a half pound between four is surprisingly filling). Finally we agreed to head north by northeast until we caught sight of the river. After a mile or two the hot wind began to blow stronger than before and the sky became overcast.

'Big fire over there,' Chilbi called.

Far off in the direction from which the wind was blowing, great clouds of smoke rose hundreds of feet into the air. They were at least ten miles away, but the wind was in our direction, blowing the fire across plains of long dry grass at a speed we estimated would be about ten miles an hour. We, on the other hand, could make only three or four miles an hour, and the river was not yet in sight. While there was no need for panic as yet, there was no time for a rest either.

A massive cloud of smoke from a bushfire billows up into the sky. The effects of a big fire are devastating, laying waste hundreds of square miles of grassland. ▼

We moved faster, pushing the camels as hard as we could, our calf muscles aching and our feet starting to blister with the unaccustomed lengthy strides. Our progress halted abruptly at an anti-dingo fence. There was no gate in sight and now was not the time to go and find one. Stripping to the waist Paddy and I attacked the fence with a pair of pliers each, led the camels through and hastily retensioned the wires and sewed the mesh back. We timed ourselves from whoa to go: sixteen minutes, or a delay of one mile at the present pace. Both of us had worked at fencing at some time in our pasts, and I surveyed our handiwork with pride.

'Reckon that'll keep the dogs out for 'em?' I asked Paddy.

'Dogs, pigs, tourists, it'll keep the bloody lot out.'

It was another hard hour's travel before the river line came in sight on our left, but several fence lines stood between us and the river. We kept on our present bearing, pausing briefly at a waterhole surrounded by lovely little kurrajong trees. Their leaves are green and shiny and make wonderful browse; their seeds can be roasted to make passable coffee; their wood burns excellently; and Aborigines use their bark fibre for fishing nets and their roots as an emergency water supply. You could not ask more than that from just one little tree.

Slowly our tension eased as we realised the fire was not making enough headway to overtake us.

Late in the afternoon we stumbled out of the long grass onto a bitumen road, heading straight across to the river about four miles away. We decided that although Burke and Wills probably did not follow the route of this road, we certainly would. The fire could overtake us if we camped this side of the river. The bitumen itself was very hard on camels' pads but the bore drain alongside the road—designed to take the run-off during the wet—was good going, and it was along this we plodded, the pace slowing down now that our goal was in sight.

We climbed back briefly onto the road to avoid a stony gully, emerging onto the bitumen at the same time as a mud-splattered pick-up truck appeared from nowhere at terrifying speed, braking unevenly to halt a few yards ahead of us. A beard appeared out of the window, mostly hidden by a wide tattered hat. 'Shift those bloody yaks,' its owner yelled by way of greeting.

The car door opened and a long angular body appeared below the beard. I approached, tired and cranky and quite ready to exchange unpleasantries with this ragged stranger. I had drawn close when he reached out, punched me on the

The team, with the author leading the way on foot, travel along a bitumen road to escape a bushfire that was making its way towards them with alarming speed. ▼

shoulder and laughed. 'G'day you old bugger. You're still picking lousy damned horses!' I recognised the voice finally: it was an old friend, a Gulf Country veterinarian known to his friends as The Chopper. He had heard rumours in one stock camp or another that we were heading this way and had driven down on the chance that our paths might cross and we could pause long enough to boil a billy.

He accompanied us across the creek, where we found a good campsite not far off the road. While we unloaded the camels and got the fire going, he shooed his dog off a pile of tarpaulins in the back of the pick-up, and from beneath the pile he produced fresh beef and a dozen hot cans of beer. 'Kimberley cold' he called them. We sat around the fire as the beef roasted, passing the billy and the yarns round. After the meal The Chopper rose and said he had better be going as he was due to start TB-testing a herd of cattle in the Northern Territory— 250 miles away—at dawn the next day. With a quiet 'Be seein' yer mate' he disappeared into the darkness.

We crawled into our swags and for a while I lay awake watching the moon shining blood red through the haze of the distant bushfire, occasionally obscured by the ominous pall of black smoke. I dozed off, dreaming of bushfires all night.

A noisy group of grey apostle birds heralded in the dawn, the sun rising reddened and enlarged by the haze. Despite their shrill piety we remained in our swags. We had agreed we would have to make a day's stop to lance and drain Cleo's pack sore. At last, driven by the need for a cuppa, I crawled reluctantly out, threw a bit of kindling onto the coals of last night's fire and wandered down to the creek to fill the billy. Curtains of thick green algae floated on the shallow pool, and the sleepy head of a turtle appeared briefly through the slime. Although it was far from appealing, the water would be all right once it was boiled.

Freshwater turtles like these, lined up as if preparing to dive in unison, are found in rivers, lakes and swamps throughout northern and eastern Australia. They are sometimes referred to as tortoises to distinguish them from their marine counterparts. ▼

I filled the billy and headed back to camp. It was a tranquil setting—the thin smoke of our fire drifting up through the silver–grey leaves of the ironbark grove, four motionless adventurers relaxing on upturned saddles and gazing idly into the fire, totally at peace with life. The Australian bush might not appeal to everyone—it might seem drab when compared with the autumn colours of Vermont hillsides or the green of the Vienna woods—but it did offer the illusion of an endless peace. Once again the lassitude of the rest day set in, the drone of flies and the trill of cicadas blending with the murmur of voices round the campfire.

By lunchtime Cleo had been treated, our chores were finished, and we headed off for some barramundi fishing in a nearby waterhole. Huge Papuan ghost gums shaded the thirty-foot-high banks lining the river, a beautiful sweep of deep water on which pelicans and other waterfowl abounded. There were heads and backbones of huge 'barra' everywhere on the banks, but of live ones we saw not the smallest nibble. I remarked that a beautiful stretch of water like this was an ideal habitat for the freshwater crocodile, a remark which I think Frankie may have overheard, for he sat back from the water with his fishing line trailing limply.

After an hour of fruitless casting Paddy and I decided to give it up and go for a swim. Clothes off, we plunged into the cold water and washed off the sweat of the trip. As we splashed about Frankie let out a yell: he had a bite. We trod water while we watched him haul a small catfish to the shore and, taking no chances with crocs, pull it slowly up the thirty-foot bank.

The night was so hot that I slept on top of my swag wearing only shorts. Some time in the early hours I woke up freezing cold. Dark clouds hid the moon and a strong wind had come up. I crawled inside my swag, pulling the canvas flap up over my head, and slept once more. What seemed only minutes later Chilbi was gently shaking me awake.

'Sun up, boss. Camels gone.'

We searched for hours. At one point I spotted tracks which Chilbi, in front of me, had clearly missed. I called him back to show him, a touch of pride in my voice. 'That track yesterday morning,' he said quietly, and continued on up the creek. I followed, somewhat crestfallen.

We found Cleo and Frances a long way off, while Paddy and Frankie found the others on the far side of the creek—they must have crossed it early in the morning.

▲ These young Aboriginal fishermen look justifiably delighted with their day's catch of barramundi—some of which are almost as big as they are! The little boy to the left of the picture is holding up the spear with which they were caught.

We saddled up and hit the road again, heading up a rocky rise thick with sucker regrowth (new shoots emerging after a bushfire), wood swallows and apostle birds heaping scorn on our intrusion. This regrowth gave way after a few hours to an open treeless plain, and here we paused for lunch beneath a solitary bean tree, trying to sing a very wild and wary Brahman-cross heifer into our tucker-bag for tea. We were out of luck again, so mounted up and headed north.

The plain gave way to a blue peppermint forest growing out of a bed of red clay, raised into numerous tombstones by termites. Between the tombstones grew spinifex and patches of scrawny native grasses. After some miles of this, with a plague of locusts thrown in, we entered better country: tall eucalypts, bean trees and a scrub resembling mulga bush on the banks of Murdering Creek, which crossed our path to empty out into the Cloncurry River. Here a large boar fell to our gun, and around midafternoon Paddy brought down an emu.

We intended to camp that night at an old mustering camp shown on the map as Monkey Hut, which suggested that we might be able to camp indoors—a good thing, as black clouds were gathering. We reached Monkey Hut at nightfall, but the hut had an unpleasant smell about it—due, it turned out, to a dead dog under the verandah. We moved off and set up camp alongside the nearby cattle yards. Dark clouds gathered as we ate, and spots of rain seemed to herald an approaching storm. Around us we could hear pigs rustling, the quiet night pierced occasionally by their squeals and squabbles.

As we had made our way north along the river the thought had struck me that while Wills had sketched the creek accurately on his map, he had given

The Fire of Life

FIRE IS ONE OF THE GREAT paradoxes of Nature. It is at once the most destructive of the four ancient elements, leaving in its wake a trail of death and devastation, and yet it can also be a prerequisite for life itself.

In the Australian outback, where tinder-dry plants bake under a relentless sun, bushfires are a common occurrence. But for some plants, far from spelling disaster, bushfires are actually a necessity. For the evergreen shrub Banksia, the heat of a bushfire acts as a signal to its fire-resistant seed cones. After the flames have passed, the cones open, releasing their seeds onto clear ground covered with fertile ash—ideal conditions for growth. Certain types of eucalyptus tree, too, respond to the intense heat

of fire, which stimulates dormant leaf-buds lying under their bark. Eucalypts also protect themselves from severe burning by having highly flammable leaves. These burn fiercely but so quickly that no damage is done to the sapwood beneath the tree's bark. Other plants, like young grass trees, suffer greatly in bushfires, but grow at such a rate that their charred stumps are transformed in a matter of weeks.

Not all bushfires start accidentally. In a practice sometimes known as fire-stick farming, the Aborigines have for thousands of years set controlled bushfires to ensure the new growth of plants essential to their diet, and to create open-forest and scrub habitats that attract the animals they hunt for food.

▲ **The immediate aftermath of a bushfire is a scene of total devastation. But on the banksias (the large shrubs in the middle ground) seed cones have started to open.**

bearings—based on his star observations—most of which were about the same distance east of the creek. Long after the expedition was over I returned to the Department of Crown Lands and Survey in Melbourne and checked Wills's map in their vault. Each bearing given was indeed six or seven miles east of the river.

Magnetic variation—my earlier explanation for quirks in the route—was starting to sound too glib; there had to be another explanation. I discussed the matter later with Rick Bailey, a navigator in the Navy, who contended that such a consistent error was probably due to a fault in the chronometer used to time star observations. A constant error of six miles to the east would most likely result from the clock's being twenty-four seconds fast—which would have been very possible, due to the bumping it had received on the back of a camel or even to the temperature extremes they had encountered.

Intrigued by this, I checked all Wills's bearings back to the mountains and discovered something very interesting. Of the ten camps, eight were given bearings six miles east of the Corella River, one five miles east and one eight miles east. This would suggest—allowing for the error with the chronometer—that Burke *had* in fact followed the Corella, not the Cloncurry. Harry Towner had been right. I noticed something else on the map to confirm this conclusion. Wills had sketched in mountains to the west of Camp 104 and a larger mountain to the east. At the latitude he gave for this camp (20°21'40" south) there are no mountains west of the Cloncurry, but on the Corella River not only do mountains stand to the west but the larger Mount Malakoff stands to the east, just as in his sketch. Thus the question of Burke's route through this region seemed eventually

▲ This picture was taken at the same scene seven weeks later. Already the grass trees have put out foot-high shoots from their charred stumps.

▲ Thirteen weeks after the fire, the grass trees now have abundant new growth, and the eucalyptus trees in the background have fresh young leaves on their trunks.

to have been resolved. At the time, though, without Wills's map, we still could not be sure, but we cared little that night as we dozed in the light drizzle.

From Monkey Hut to Paddy's Lagoon

When Chilbi and I set out to retrieve the camels in the pre-dawn light we could make out the vague shapes of pigs retreating to their daytime haunts. While most of Australia's wild pigs are certainly descended from domestic European pigs gone wild, it is widely held by hunters that there exists, in the Gulf and on Cape York, a larger and more ferocious pig known as the Captain Cooker. This is believed to descend from Asian pigs released when Cook's *Endeavour* went aground. They are said to be high at the withers (or shoulder) and low at the rump, with enormous tusks and vile tempers—a type of super-pig. Cook's journal did record some pigs escaping and there were some very big pigs up here, but they didn't seem to differ much in shape from pigs further south. They tasted much the same, too.

The sun rose, penetrating the murky sky enough to reveal the camels' tracks heading off towards a large patch of gidgee scrub, where we found them kneeling down and ruminating quietly after their night's feeding.

We left Monkey Hut and its dog, and after miles of thick regrowth scrub we abruptly hit flat, open country. The going was good—black-soil plains with fat cattle pausing to stare at us—until Dismal Creek. On the other side of the creek (which seemed no more dismal than many) the country became heavily wooded, with stony outcrops. Progress slowed accordingly. This was a particularly bone-jarring twenty miles. My back soon became so sore that I could barely sit on a camel for even the shortest spell, and walking became a blessed relief.

Emerging suddenly into a clearing we came upon a swath of forest half a mile wide. The trees, some of which must have stood forty or fifty feet high, had been totally flattened, all of them lying in the same direction. The ruin extended for a couple of miles, total destruction then giving way within a few paces to normal undisturbed forest. It was almost impossible to envisage any force that could confine so much damage to so discrete an area.

Descending from the high country with its unexplained mystery we struck the river flats, black soil covered in thorn-bush thickets ten feet high and seemingly endless, with cattle tracks and erosion gullies our only means through. Several miles of this saw us turn wearily back to higher ground to the west where the sun was now sinking low towards the horizon.

At dusk, after much searching, we spotted the outbuildings of Cowan Downs. The station was set on a barren hill of undulating red rock, a surrealistic lunar landscape made more weird by ghost gums which seemed to grow out of the solid rock. The homestead itself was a rambling two-storey building looking out over the plains. An atmosphere of old-world charm and rustic comfort prevailed there despite years of neglect.

Our hosts, the new owners David and Marcela, insisted that we all sleep inside 'in one of the dormitories' and since the clouds overhead looked ready to burst we readily accepted. Showered and scrubbed with teeth clean and fresh socks on, we felt like new men as we sat down to eat. At that moment two stockmen appeared at the door, one holding his eye in obvious pain. He had been welding up a bore when a spark flew into his eye. I sat him under the kitchen light and rinsed the eye out, revealing a small gash on the cornea and a tiny metal chip beneath the eyelid. A torchlight search of our medical bag outside in the pouring rain produced one half-squashed tube of the appropriate ointment, enough to relieve pain until he could get to a doctor.

Otherwise the night passed pleasantly, with lively talk around the big dinner table in an air of warm old-fashioned hospitality, while the rain beat on the windowpanes and beds with clean sheets awaited us upstairs. We were not long in reaching them.

Next morning, about four miles north of the homestead, we found ourselves on an extraordinary lava flow, wide and devoid of growth except for a solitary species of tree which—like the dwarf eucalyptus of the previous day—again grew straight out of the rock. This tree was unlike any I had seen: the trunk had smooth bark and was bloated like a bottle tree. It supported a handful of large green leaves and bright yellow flowers which exuded the strangest odour; its apple-sized fruit were not really appealing either.

No entry was made in Wills's diary during the original trip up through this region. But on the return journey there were a number of entries, just sufficient to enable us to pinpoint their whereabouts. On February 24, 1861, for example, Wills recorded their progress down a creek which crept along 'at the foot of the ranges'. Sure enough, to our west, close on the river, stood Donor's Hills—not a great range to a cartographer and thus omitted from most maps, but a significant range from a camel train's viewpoint.

That night we made camp about one mile from Donor's Hill Station. Then, pushing on, we lunched level with the junction of the Cloncurry and Flinders rivers, the latter referred to by Wills as a 'branch creek with running water'.

Ahead, a spur of the Donor's Hills range loomed up, forcing the river to bend round to the east. An old Cobb and Co coach track went up over the spur, and to save a few miles we decided to take it. (In 1853 an American, Freeman Cobb, began a coaching company in Melbourne and soon introduced a fast, light stagecoach to link the goldfields and the cities. Despite competition

▲ This colourful Cobb and Co coach plied its trade in Victoria in the late 19th century. Before the advent of railways in Australia, such coaches were the only means of long-distance travel for the general public.

from the railways, the company expanded across Australia, only finally ceasing operations in 1924.)

Here and there the rut marks of the old coaches could still be seen on the stony path as it rose steeply above the tall green timber to a level plateau paved in red gravel. From here the entire river plain below was visible, long green ribbons winding across a vast yellow landscape. Our descent to the plains on the other side was rough going, the weight of the packs forcing the camels down so fast they had no chance of a safe footing and slid much of the way.

The black-soil plains, which had seemed quite flat when viewed from the plateau, proved to be cracked by the heat into gilgais and broken up further by the hooves of cattle. It was far from easy going. We crossed to a line of trees which marked a series of billabongs, almost certainly the billabongs along which Burke travelled by moonlight on February 23, returning from the Gulf. Seeing one marked Paddy's Lagoon on the map, we headed across to camp for the night so that Paddy could see his lagoon. It was muddy and he was not impressed.

I slept poorly that night, my brain endlessly calculating rations and mileages, and wrestling with the problem of keeping the camels going at this pace. The likely outcome of any attempt to return before spelling the poor beasts—resting them thoroughly—was dire.

We were woken at dawn by a blood-chilling yell from Chilbi.

The previous night the talk had centred on reports of a nineteen-foot croc which had recently swallowed a man up north somewhere. The attack had apparently taken place at a billabong not much bigger than the one on which we were camped. As I was telling the story I noticed a few anxious eyes searching the surface of the lagoon for anything that resembled a waiting crocodile, but only a couple of black-tailed water hens disturbed the stillness. I noticed too that everyone (myself included) placed their swags so that the fire stood between them and the waterhole, and the fire was considerably larger than usual.

▲ Not Paddy's muddy lagoon but one very similar. This is Combo Waterhole, immortalised as the billabong in the folk song 'Waltzing Matilda'.

Chilbi's yell had us instantly awake, grabbing for pants, boots and rifle in that order. He had awoken at dawn after dreaming of crocs all night, and had felt something cold and scaly moving beside him under the blanket. We slowly lifted the blanket to reveal a tree goanna. Relieved and feeling slightly ridiculous we uncocked the rifle and sat down to tell and retell the story, laughing more and more with each telling.

We were laughing still as we saddled up and set out, but the laughter soon died down as we struck a black-soil plain chopped into a million potholes by the hooves of cattle during the wet. The rough surface was hidden by waist-high grass so we constantly tripped as we struggled slowly northward. It was impossible to ride, for the camels could not get into their smooth, swinging stride. In addition, our path was crossed by numerous sharp erosion gullies forcing us to detour frequently.

It was a great relief when a road crossed our path and for a while we could step out along it without falling into invisible sinkholes. Our relief was short-lived, however, for the road veered east and we reluctantly had to leave it and head northwards. Here, though, the grass had been swept away in a recent bushfire, so at least the sinkholes could now be seen and avoided.

The heat was intense and the air so heavy with moisture that our clothes were soon drenched, while our boots squelched as we walked. We took advantage of the lunch break to empty our boots out, a rather foul odour greeting us as we did, overpowering the gamy smell of overripe roo tail. Boots on and bellies full we pushed on again, travelling across the plain parallel to the Flinders River.

Finally, after travelling over thirty miles, we halted on the plain, lit a few sticks to boil the billy and lay down too exhausted to cook a meal. After half an hour Paddy recovered enough to dampen a handful of oats to eat, and I tried chewing a stick of biltong but gave it up as being too much like hard work.

We lay back, drained, watching the gaunt shapes of the camels heading towards the setting sun in search of browse. They moved slowly now, ribs and hips plainly visible, a pack sore on Walloper's right hip giving him an uneven gait. With the Gulf of Carpentaria only a day's march away I found myself staring at bitter reality and sat sadly watching my theory go west with the limping camels. By tomorrow we would be half way, but already we had taken fifty-two of the eighty-four days Burke had allowed for the trip, and there was no way camels in this condition could turn around tomorrow and make it back to Cooper Creek in the thirty-two remaining.

We had set out confident that we could do what Burke had failed to achieve, going from Cooper Creek to the Gulf and back in twelve weeks, which would mean averaging twenty-two miles a day, six days a week. We had tried to maintain this speed, but the effect on the camels was now clearly visible, even though they were only half-loaded. Their humps, once well-filled stores of energy-rich fat reserves, were now all but absent, hipbones and ribs were covered only by skin, and more pack sores were inevitable. The stony plains and sandstone ranges had led to the pads of their feet becoming worn and bruised. Our camels were approaching the state of exhaustion that cameleers called *founder*, described by an old camel hand, Major Glynn, in 1894, as 'a kind of dropsy, or poorness and thinness of the blood produced by overwork and absence of proper food'.

▲ Paddy snatches 40 winks on a none-too-comfortable camel mattress, but the camels don't seem to mind.

On Greg's trip from Alice Springs to Gulgong, a journey of 1,600 miles, his camels had covered twenty miles a day, but at each town he came to he spelled them for a week or so; thus their average distance per day over the entire journey was much reduced. It seemed then that it was the rate of walking which wore camels down more than the weight they carried; it was not 'the final straw' which broke the camel's back, but rather an extra five miles covered each day.

I was later to find other evidence that this is indeed the case. Wilfred Thesiger, whose writings I found only after the trip, was one of the very few Westerners ever to be fully accepted by the Bedouin tribesmen of Arabia; he managed to join up with El Rashid, the 'Wolves of the Desert', generally regarded as some of the most knowledgeable camel men on earth, desert raiders who will cover a hundred miles in a single ride.

In 1948 Thesiger accompanied them on an epic crossing of the 'dead quarter' of the Arabian desert. They covered the 1,140-odd miles to Abu Dhabi at a slightly slower pace than ours (twenty miles a day), but with their camels similarly loaded. (They considered the loads of 200 pounds or so heavy as they preferred to travel light and fast, over shorter distances.) The El Rashid guides told Thesiger that carrying these loads at this pace the camels would without doubt develop saddlesores and possibly founder before they covered the distance. These desert tribes must have understood the importance of loads and pace long before—probably centuries before—we set out.

I was later (oh, the advantages of hindsight!) to come across a rare copy of A.S. Leese's book on camel medicine. He was a veterinarian whose expertise in camels came from years of experience. He wrote:

> 'An average distance for a day's march is fifteen miles...for properly managed camels relying on grazing only and getting no rations. Under conditions of active service longer daily average distances can be done, but it is an abuse of the camel, and permanent transport cannot be kept efficient that way. A common fault with European officers with camels is to be in too much of a hurry...'

In this last sentence Leese might well have been referring to Landells, Burke's 'camel expert', who covered the 600 miles from Peshawar to Karachi at fifty miles a day with pack camels!

The facts of the matter lay clearly before me. Burke had set out to do twenty-two miles a day, but had not been able to maintain that rate. I had set out to show that, with lighter loads and in the right season, it was possible. I had shown the *opposite*. Even with modern medical care, and the occasional benefit of roads and tracks, our camels clearly could never have kept up such a pace for long enough. Thus the delays Burke would later strike, caused by the wet season, were *not* of paramount importance. His camels would have knocked up in any season.

It was a strange moment for me, sitting on the plain, knowing that two years of preparation and nearly 1,000 miles of dust and sweat had done little other than prove me wrong.

Across the burnt-out plain the sun finally set, and my spirits were lifted by the most extraordinary sunset I have ever witnessed, the sky glowing red, gold, green and blue in slow succession while two small pure-white clouds floated across it. Gradually the blue turned to purple which steadily deepened until the first stars appeared. The peace and sheer beauty of it pushed aside all thoughts of defeat. I watched it for a long time in silence, then fell asleep dreaming of camels walking well fed, happy and healthy all the way back to the Dig Tree.

My dreams disappeared in the light of dawn, replaced by our own faithful beasts who slowly knelt to receive their burdens yet again, roaring their disgust at life in general and us in particular.

We plodded across the plain, with Walloper and Ginger pulling back, both leg-sore and weary. A bore loomed up in the distance and we made for it, noting a mob of wild pigs around it as we drew closer. Paddy stalked them into nearby scrub, shooting one as they disappeared. Abruptly it turned and went for him, only a few feet separating them until his second shot dropped it in its tracks. It was a very near thing!

We paused at the bore to water the camels and cut up the pig, then set off towards the river, lined now by thick forest and, closer in, by mangroves. On the far side of the river from us stood a series of low sandstone bluffs, originally discovered by Ludwig Leichhardt who had crossed the river here fifteen years before Burke. Wills had read the journals of earlier expeditions through this northern region, and he knew that the country ahead had already been explored, if briefly and unsuccessfully, by the British. Indeed he and Burke had crossed the path of earlier explorers the day before, and thus Burke had already fulfilled his brief by finding a route to the known country in the north. Had he turned back here he would have saved precious days, for the wet season was to set in and catch him on the black-soil plains. But Burke had to be the first man to cross the entire continent and there was no talk of turning back. King later told of their passing stony ridges south of their Camp 119. By this time they must have been on the other side of the river.

We decided to cross and pushed through the thick forest, our progress held up by lianas, fallen logs and chest-high cane grass. At last we reached a narrow belt of mangroves, through which lay a pebble beach and beyond it a broad sweep of river, fifty yards wide. On the far shore a group of pelicans eyed us passively, while nearby two green–black cormorants stood sunning themselves. We made our way down to the shore but when the camels began to sink into the mud we retreated, content to walk along the pebble flat in search of a crossing.

A forest of aerial roots lines the shore of a mangrove swamp in Queensland. The roots are an adaptation to living in waterlogged, oxygen-poor soils, allowing the trees to absorb extra oxygen from the atmosphere. ▼

We noticed something on the beach and wandered over to find the four-foot-long bill of a sawfish edged—as its name would suggest—in sharp teeth. This fascinated Chilbi and Frankie; it took me quite a while to explain to Frankie what a sawfish was, and therefore why we would rather not cross the river here. We pushed back into the woodland which skirted the river. Passing a little south of a billabong I saw something floating in the water. We watched it for a little while, a small, partly submerged log which hung motionless, its yellow pupils taking in our every move. Not at all the frightening monster we had dreamed of, but a three-foot croc nonetheless.

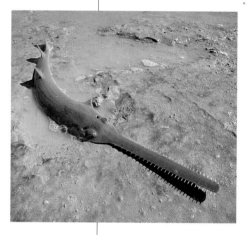

We finally crossed the creek by means of the concrete causeway on the Burketown road, and no more than a mile from the road we pulled up on the eastern bank of the river. Around us stood a circle of gnarled old box trees. Some were now dead, but each one bore a mark, or blaze, made a long time ago, the blazes in most cases almost overgrown. Called before a court of enquiry, King had told how Burke's party had blazed some fifteen small box trees at Camp 119. We had reached their northernmost camp.

▲ The sawfish uses its toothed bill to cut swaths through schools of fish by shaking its head violently from side to side. This kills several fish at one go, which the sawfish then eats.

Wearily we unpacked the camels, noting as we did so that Walloper's sores were worse than ever, and Ginger was starting to go the same way. We agreed that the camels would have to spell for a couple of weeks to regain strength and let the pack sores heal before they could face that journey again. But two weeks were more than Burke could have spared: he had food problems and a narrow schedule to keep. He had people depending on his swift return. So had we. Having taken nearly two months to get up here there was no way we could make the return journey in just one. At this point, after everything we had all gone through, reality finally had to be faced: this was the end for us. Our trip was over.

Of Burke and Bergin

Paddy and I made the trip up to Saltwater Creek, a tidal stream fifteen-odd miles north of Camp 119 where Burke and Wills had left King and Grey to look after the camels, and had headed for the sea taking only Billy, the horse. But then the wet had set in and the horse floundered in the mud and rain, so they hobbled it and continued towards the Gulf on foot.

They were now in the land of the Yappar people, gentle fisherfolk who lived in two-storey thatched huts resembling giant beehives, people who had kindly guided the explorer Leichhardt across the river twenty years earlier. They were not changed much in 1861:

'Here we passed three blacks who, as is universally their custom, pointed out to us unasked the best path down. This assisted us greatly.'

Despite their help, Burke's hopes of reaching the sea were dashed. He found himself blocked by mangroves and flood plains, and had to turn back. Standing there together in that lonely spot, Paddy and I could only sympathise with Burke and the enormity of the task which had then faced him. Burke had only

▲ Land gives way to meandering rivers, which finally disgorge into the sea at the Gulf of Carpentaria. This very landscape defeated Burke and Wills, and when the author too came upon it, he understood why.

twenty-seven days' provisions left, with little chance of supplementing them off the land, and since he had taken fifty-seven days to reach the Gulf when relatively fit and well provisioned, he could hardly hope to make the return journey in less than half that time. One camel was already lost and the others were leg-weary and in need of rest, and on top of it all they would be caught in the wet on the black-soil plains.

Can Burke be blamed for planning his trip to the Gulf at the rate of twenty-two miles a day rather than the fifteen miles a day that is all that camels can reasonably maintain? This was the first camel expedition in Australia, and Landells, the 'camel expert', had boasted of his trip with camels from Peshawar to Karachi at fifty miles a day; Burke cannot be blamed for heeding the words of the only camel expert available, but rather should be commended for taking the word of this rogue with a grain of salt.

Burke will forever remain one of the paradoxes of Australian exploration, for his errors were, on the one hand, his indecision and, on the other, his all-engulfing, single-minded determination. His major error came when he said 'perhaps' on three occasions, for on an exercise of this magnitude there was no room for doubt. He told Wright that his appointment *might* be confirmed or that another officer *might* arrive to lead the relief expedition. He told Wright and Brahe that he *might* send a team of pack camels back to Menindee to help bring up supplies. He told Brahe that he *might* get picked up by a vessel in the Gulf or head for Queensland instead of returning to Cooper Creek. No general tells his infantry commander that he may perhaps send cavalry to support the left flank, or that he may perhaps direct his artillery fire in a certain direction. The seeds of doubt are deadly for they double the number of contingencies.

His other error was in direct contrast to this: his decisiveness, his stubborn determination to win the glory of the first crossing to the Gulf, to keep going when his supplies were half gone, and his readiness to starve rather than alter course, all contributed equally to his downfall.

Wills wrote, in his last letter, 'The great dryness and scarcity of game and our forced marching prevented us from supplying the deficiency from external sources to any great extent.' Burke's haste had put them fatally out of step with the environment.

The Lessons of the Desert

The next day found us sitting at the bar of the Purple Pub in Normanton. Chilbi and Frankie were looking forward to their trip in the plane back to Alice Springs, and I was booked on a flight to Brisbane the next day. John Barnes, the manager of Magowra station, was that day sending a truck across to Townsville in Queensland, and had kindly offered to take our camels. From there, after a spell, they were to be sent by rail down to Gulgong, in the care of Paddy.

Paddy, in his usual determined fashion, would gladly have waited a few more weeks for the camels to improve, then done the return leg of our trip living off the bush as best he could, just to complete what we had set out to do. I dissuaded him. The true purpose of our trip had already been accomplished; to endure any more hardships would have been pure masochism.

In seven weeks we had covered roughly 1,000 miles, only to find that my theory did not fit the facts. Although I was disappointed I could not help but feel that the venture had not been entirely worthless.

Physically we had come through well and, although I had lost about twenty-five pounds in weight, I still felt in good shape. Mentally we had overcome personal and cultural differences to weld together into a close-knit team. Above all, we now had a much better idea of the route Burke and Wills had taken and of the problems they had faced.

My feelings, inevitably, were mixed. I felt disappointed (to be proved wrong), ashamed (to have let down Paddy and everyone else who had believed in me), and guilty (for the sufferings of the camels). I also, less worthily, felt angry in advance at all the armchair critics who had sat back and said I wouldn't make it, and who would now be able to congratulate themselves and snigger.

But against all this there was something else. Inside myself I had been changed for ever. It was an incredible sensation. I had breathed desert air and lived closer to the realities of existence than I had ever dared dream possible. I had not just watched this. I had not driven past the ancient world of rock and sand, of raging sun and bitter moonlight. I had walked it, felt it, lived it. I would not be the same.

The desert was now an old friend, a refuge if I ever needed one in the future, and I felt quite extraordinarily alive. I also felt a sense of achievement, to have walked in Burke's footsteps. I had earned the right to judge him, I thought, and had learned enough through my own mistakes to be able to judge him fairly.

Preparing to Go

Options For those planning a visit to Australia, a range of options is available. Package tours save time and effort, and can take in cities, hikes, wildlife tours and diving trips. For the independent traveller, motels, private hotels, hostels, bed and breakfast and accommodation on working farms are on offer. Campsites are found near almost all tourist areas, and some have cabins for hire.

Travel Most international airlines fly to Australia's principal cities. Those flying from Europe often have stopovers in Southeast Asia. Distances within Australia are so huge that it is best either to restrict a stay to one or two states or to use internal flights. The bus network is reasonably comprehensive, covering far more places than the railways. Passes for rail and bus travel are available (mostly purchased in Australia), allowing unlimited journeys within a given period. Hiring or buying a car or camper van obviously gives more freedom of movement. In the outback, most roads except for main highways are little more than dirt tracks, and distances between towns can be vast. Travellers should always carry ample drinking water and, in case they break down, tell someone where they are going. Note that driving through Central Australia in summer can be dangerously hot, for both passengers and vehicle.

Practicalities Visas, lasting three or six months, are needed for all visitors except New Zealanders. One-year working-holiday visas are available to nationals of certain countries, mainly for those aged under 26. On arrival, visitors must be able to show they have sufficient funds for the duration of their stay as well as a ticket for onward travel. Vaccinations are not required unless, within the two weeks prior to arrival, travellers have visited areas affected by yellow fever, cholera or typhus.

When to go The Australian summer runs from December to March, the seasons being the reverse of those in the Northern Hemisphere; winter is between June and August. Spring and autumn are the best times to travel. The tropical north has its rainy season in summer, when many roads are washed out. Tasmania, in the south, has a temperate

climate and is best visited in summer. Western Australia has spectacular wild flowers in spring. The Snowy Mountains, near Canberra, and parts of Victoria receive plentiful winter snow—more in fact than the European Alps.

Health hazards The dangers of excessive exposure to the sun are taken very seriously. Even in cloudy conditions high-factor sun lotion is essential. Visitors should avoid prolonged exposure to the sun and beware of dehydration and sunstroke. Swimmers in tropical waters should be on guard for jellyfish, sea wasps, sea snakes and sharks; saltwater crocodiles are found in estuaries. Coastal rock pools further south are home to the deadly blue-ringed octopus. Venomous snakes and spiders are potential hazards in many areas. Lifesavers and planes patrol popular beaches for sharks and other dangers.

Specialist activities Much of the finest **hiking** or 'bushwalking' is in the south of the mainland and Tasmania. Details can be found in guidebooks. Marked trails exist in many areas, including the Blue Mountains and the Snowy Mountains. Long-distance trails crisscross the great mainland expanses, some passing through eucalyptus forests, others taking in mountains. Walkers need to be very fit and well equipped to attempt these. Many coastal waters are outstanding for **water sports** such as surfing, sailing and diving. Equipment is often available locally, and scuba-diving schools operate

on and around the Great Barrier Reef. Scuba divers must not venture into the depths alone without training. **Camel treks** are available at various centres in the desert, including Alice Springs.

Where to Go

Australian Capital Territory Canberra, Australia's capital, lies roughly halfway between Sydney and Melbourne. The city is interesting for, among other things, its planned layout dating from 1912, and the outstanding art collection in the Australian National Gallery.

New South Wales No visitor should miss Sydney, with its vibrant, cosmopolitan atmosphere, famous beaches, excellent cultural attractions and waterfront—with the Sydney Harbour Bridge and Opera House. The city's hinterland includes the Blue Mountains, a dramatic sandstone escarpment, with waterfalls, rugged cliffs, splendid caves and excellent walks. Boats can be hired at Brooklyn for exploring the unspoilt scenery of the Hawkesbury River. North of Sydney the Hunter Valley is a major wine-producing region, and wines can be sampled at most vineyards.

Northern Territory The territory's capital, Darwin, is in the lush terrain of the far north. Much of the rest of the territory is arid. Uluru, or Ayers Rock, 1,142 feet high and six miles round, is the territory's premier attraction. It can be climbed in an hour, but many prefer to